Annie Bell

gorgeousdesserts

with photographs by Chris Alack

Kyle Cathie Limited

First published in Great Britain in 2007 by
Kyle Cathie Limited
122 Arlington Road, London NW1 7HP
www.kylecathie.com

ISBN 978-185626-742-7

A CIP catalogue record for this title is available from the British Library

10 9 8 7 6 5 4 3 2 1

Editor: Stephanie Evans
Design: pinkstripedesign.com
Proofreader: Sharon Brown
Indexer: Ursula Caffrey
Photographer: Chris Alack
Food Stylists: Lorna Brash, Clare Lewis, Kim Morphew, Penny Stephens
Props Stylist: Sue Radcliffe
Production: Sha Huxtable & Alice Holloway
Colour reproduction: Colourscan, Singapore
Printed and bound in Singapore by Star Standard Industries Pty Ltd

contents

introduction

Some of us could happily live off puddings, and it is only our waistline that makes us see sense. While their role is to round off lunch or dinner, desserts – like cakes or sweets – are one of life's trivial indulgences, a treat. And in our house we tend to reserve them for weekends, they are a ritual part of any Saturday and Sunday. Woe betide should I forget or forego something lovely to finish with: I am cajoled by my son who I think must count down from Monday until we get to that sweet treat. Desserts make any occasion seem more special than it might otherwise have been. So much so that to invite friends over for a meal and not go to the trouble of producing a pud almost seems rude – it is an accepted part of hospitality. And if it's a real extravaganza, then there is every reason to go to town and dish up several, a grand finale almost like a pudding buffet, and you can guarantee that everyone will insist on trying a little of each one.

sweet gorgeousness

And, again like cakes, desserts belong firmly in the realm of the home kitchen; they make mothers out of the least domestic of us. It doesn't really matter if you hate ironing, are terrible with a hoover and can't thread a needle to save your life, turn out a winning plum pie and custard and all is forgiven. At least, I like to think so. But more than that I am rarely tempted by the dessert menu in restaurants, as invariably they arrive tricked up and twee, when my idea of a pudding is something that you can sink into and wallow, a generous splash of sweet gorgeousness.

I mean the kind of puds that have 'forbidden' writ large all over them, which only adds to their allure. Big bowls of steaming fluffy chocolate sponge drowned in a salty caramel sauce, a wobbly bread and butter pud or Sussex pond pudding that spills a lavish buttery lemon sauce from a suet crust. Or a dip down through the layers of a sherry trifle, through that thick bank of syllabub to the fruit and sponge soaked in sherry and brandy below. Or a contented foray into a warm rhubarb crumble bubbling with sticky pink juices at the edges.

when less is more

But puds don't have to be this indulgent – my love of jellies grows with every summer season. They're as playful as they are sharp-witted, relying on that teasing texture. Choose from a grown-up palate of jellybean flavours, watermelon, pomegranate, orange, and more exotically campari and lemon, or blackberry with Earl Grey tea. The ultimate though is the fashion statement for Champagne jelly, captured bubbles and all that fizzes as you eat it.

Perfectly ripe fruits in season too, afforded the minimum attention, will leave you feeling sufficiently virtuous compared to what might have been. A cooling strawberry soup, fragrant slivers of melon doused with vodka, juicy black cherries dipped into chocolate fondue, or figs scattered with amaretti and grilled.

One step up from that are creamy little puds, a tingling everlasting lemon syllabub, or a towering raspberry blancmange, now that Marie Antoinette has been reinstated as a heroine. And for diehard traditionalists, a simple crème caramel, with its glassy golden surface.

And when I haven't had time to make a pud specially, then I tend to dip into the freezer for a scoop of homemade ice cream. This doesn't have to involve a machine to qualify in the luxury stakes, a dark chocolatey semifreddo for instance is no more complicated than making custard. And for those seriously lazy days there are a handful of easy cheats that rely on a few tubs of sorbet or ice cream picked up on your way round the shops, to whip up a striped Neapolitan-style ice, or a vanilla bombe that spills cherry red jam.

dressing for dinner

This couldn't be easier; it's not the type of pudding but the accessories that go with it. Ices and syllabubs can be dolled up with delicate dessert biccies – almost anything Italian or French will do. A simple compote with toasted Madeira cake is divine. And hot puds relish fancy creams, chantilly or crème fraîche laced with a little liqueur or eau-de-vie.

I have a large liqueurs cabinet reserved almost exclusively for making puddings because I love to accentuate and highlight flavours. Cointreau casts a little orange magic, Amaretto enlivens almonds, Calvados warms apples, Kirsch does it for cherries, a framboise eau-de-vie lends an accent to raspberries, and Kahlúa brings out the best in coffee. I like to combine summer berries with sweet wines and liqueurs too, berries stacked in a jar with sugar and drowned with rum are a warming excuse to eat with ice cream on a chilly evening. While the strawberries I buy out in Normandy where we have a farmhouse – Marais des Bois and Gariguettes with their intense wild strawberry scent – are just perfect steeped in chilled Sauternes or other sweet wine.

perfect presentation

Any creamy little pots, chilled custards, soufflés or mousses and jellies can be made in small coffee cups or glasses. I have a wonderful set of vintage Champagne coupes, which have long since relinquished their role of sipping fizz, that make beautiful dishes for such desserts. On a more traditional note, I swear by old-fashioned pudding basins, in fact I have stacks of these in different sizes that multi-task in the kitchen.

For trifles you want a glass bowl, some 8 centimetres deep. I rarely recommend special equipment or serving dishes, but to make a trifle in anything other than a glass bowl is like drawing the curtains when the sun's out. I love to see the way the layers fuse into each other and get acquainted as they go down. Though when you do want them to look dressier than usual, then it's off to the cake shop for some bling – shimmering crystallised flowers or silver dragees.

So choose your pud and get cooking. This is where I find myself revealing my true colours. There are those who begin with the starter and work forwards, and those who begin with the pudding and work backwards....

fab fruits

These little desserts are simple by design; there's little in the way of dressing up and fancy footwork – the fruits themselves shine through. I tend to place strawberries and cream at the heart of this genre: it's the benchmark that can range from boring to sublime. So elementary, a cliché even, that most people will actually apologise for serving them at the end of a sparkling dinner. But on fine form and in season there's little case for dishing them up in a more elaborate way, and that goes for any number of other fruits. There's no apology here for popping a few fragrant Scottish raspberries into a glass, filling it with chilled Champagne and dishing it up as a dessert. Or, steeping strawberries in Sauternes, if you want to forego the cream.

Pretty much everything else lies in the same vein: the very minimum of fuss to bring out the best in whatever gorgeous fruits you have to hand – provided that they're in season. We've become so accustomed to seeing peaches, plums and strawberries at Christmas we hardly question their appearance. But they might as well be different fruits altogether, when you compare them to their sweet and juicy summer selves. Better to call on apples and pears in winter, a fluffy chocolate sponge or a bread and butter pud, and save summer fruits for the treat that they should be.

Some fruits are almost better gently cooked than raw, such as figs, baked with a little almond-scented crumble of amaretti and butter, that relax into something halfway to jam, or plums baked in the oven, which turn lusciously fleshy and dye the sweet and sour syrup a deep purple. But as winter takes hold it's big misshapen Bramley apples that I crave, their cores cut out and filled with dried fruits and spices, which fluff up in the oven and spill out from the skin.

An excuse to finish on a high note, the raspberries cast a little of their magic into the bubbles, and themselves take on something of the wine. Another favourite ruse in this vein is to steep 750g of halved strawberries in half a bottle of chilled Sauternes or Montbazillac for an hour. Do seek out really fragrant varieties for either of these desserts, they're ones to save for in-season.

raspberries in champagne

350g raspberries
½ bottle pink or white Champagne, chilled

Serves 6

Divide the raspberries between six glasses and pour over the Champagne. First eat the raspberries with a teaspoon, and then drink the Champagne.

rumpot

Rumpot is another way of acquainting ripe summer fruit with alcohol, but you're thinking ahead to cold winter evenings, as it gets better with every month that passes. Then again if you can't wait, dip in after a couple of days.

250g raspberries
70g caster sugar
130g cherries, pitted
250ml white rum

Makes 500ml

Preheat the oven to 170°C fan/190°C/gas mark 5. Remove the seal from a ½ litre Le Parfait preserving jar, put this in the oven for 5 minutes to sterilise then allow it to cool. Place half the raspberries in the base of the jar and scatter over a third of the sugar. Layer the cherries on top, scatter over another third of the sugar, then fill the jar with the remaining raspberries and scatter over the last of the sugar. The fruit should reach the top of the jar. Pour over the rum and gently press down on the fruit to submerge it. Slip the rubber seal into place and clip the jar shut. Place in a cool dark place for several months. I turn it several times during the first 24 hours to encourage the sugar to dissolve, and then right it an hour or two later. Serve the fruit with ice cream, and you can enjoy the liquor as an after-dinner liqueur.

This is one for the autumn, blackberries and pears have a brief spell together in season, though as new varieties are developed that season grows ever longer. The rosé dyes pears a pretty shade of pink and gives them a delicious winey flavour, but it could just as well be red wine – that classically renders them a deep Renaissance hue.

pears in rosé

600ml rosé wine
175g caster sugar
7cm cinnamon stick
5cm strip of orange zest,
    removed with a potato peeler
1 bay leaf
6 pears
225g blackberries

Serves 6

Place the wine, sugar, cinnamon stick, orange zest and bay leaf in a medium pan. Bring to the boil, cover and simmer over a low heat for 15 minutes.

Meanwhile peel the pears. Add them to the pan and cover with a circle of baking paper. Bring back to a simmer and poach for 15–20 minutes or until tender, turning them over halfway through. Remove them to a bowl. Reduce the remaining syrup by a third until it is quite viscous. Pour the syrup over the fruit, leaving in the flavouring ingredients. Once cool, cover and chill for several hours, turning the pears halfway through to ensure they are evenly dyed by the syrup. The pears look beautiful served whole, but if you prefer you can quarter and core them before chilling, again stirring them halfway through.

Bring back up to room temperature for 30 minutes before eating. Remove and discard the flavouring ingredients, and stir in the blackberries.

Iles flottantes or floating islands are divinely moussey poached meringues that melt in the mouth, and they're very French, which is always a recommendation. They often arrive on a pool of almond custard, but their remit goes well beyond that, and I serve them with whatever takes my fancy: in the early summer it's poached cherries. You may like to serve a plate of lacy almond tuiles or other dessert biccies.

floating islands with cherries

Cherries

700g cherries, pitted

50g caster sugar

4½ tablespoons Calvados or brandy

Squeeze of lemon juice

Floating islands

2 large egg whites

Pinch of sea salt

50g caster sugar

Crème fraîche to serve

Serves 6

Preheat the oven to 170°C fan/190°C/gas mark 5. Place the cherries in an ovenproof bowl, sprinkle with the sugar and pour over 3 tablespoons of the Calvados or brandy. Cover with foil and cook for 1 hour, stirring them once. Strain the juices into a small saucepan and simmer to reduce by about half until you have a rich syrup. Stir in the remaining spirit and a squeeze of lemon juice, and pour back over the cherries.

To make the floating islands, which takes about 10 minutes, fill a large frying or sauté pan with water and bring it to a simmer. The water should be no more than at a trembling boil. Whisk the egg whites in a bowl with the salt. Once they are risen, gradually sprinkle over the sugar, whisking well with each addition until you have a glossy meringue.

To cook the floating islands, drop heaped tablespoons of the meringue mixture into the water using another spoon to help each one slide off – you should have six in all. Turn after 30 seconds using a slotted spatula and cook for another 30 seconds. Remove and drain them on kitchen paper or a clean tea towel. The cherries should still be warm; if you've cooked them in advance gently reheat them.

To serve, place a meringue in six shallow bowls. Spoon the cherries and syrup around each île flottante, with some crème fraîche in the centre.

Here chilled cubes of fragrant ripe melon are macerated in vodka. The idea is to have three different melons and to play on their different characters, and you could also stir in some raspberries before serving. It's thirst-quenching hot-weather fare – a good one for a barbecue – that doubles in quantity with little extra effort and sits chilling in the fridge until you're ready.

chilled melon medley in vodka

½ Cantaloupe melon
   (about 600g)
½ Honeydew melon
   (about 600g)
¼ small watermelon
   (about 800g)
200ml vodka
200g raspberries (optional)

Serves 4–6

Cut the skin off each chunk of melon, taking care to remove the hard outer pale flesh as well. Scoop out the seeds from the Cantaloupe and Honeydew and cut the fruit into 2cm dice. Cut the watermelon into 2cm slices, scoop out any seeds and then dice it. Combine the melon in a large bowl, pour over the vodka, cover and chill overnight, stirring once or twice.

Just before serving, stir the raspberries if using into the chilled melon and enjoy with the juices poured over.

Nothing challenging here, just a gentle warm milk chocolate cream to dip into, which will have children clamouring for their daily portions of fruit. You can always use orange juice instead of brandy.

cherries with chocolate fondue

200g milk chocolate (e.g. Lindt),
    broken into pieces
1 tbsp brandy or dark rum
125ml single cream
900g cherries

Serves 6

Gently melt the chocolate in a bowl set over a pan with a little simmering water in it. Add the brandy or rum and single cream and whisk until smooth. Transfer to a bowl and serve with the cherries to dip into it. The fondue can also be made in advance, in which case leave to cool, then cover and chill, and gently rewarm as though melting chocolate.

hot buttered cherries

I first ate this memorable dessert at the Auberge de Cassagne in Avignon, in Provence, a simple recipe for these beautiful fruits that the chef kindly demonstrated. Melt about 100g unsalted butter and 100g caster sugar together in a large frying pan. Once it is seething add 2 tablespoons kirsch or other fruit eau-de-vie, and simmer for a minute until the sauce is smooth. Add 750g cherries and cook for 5 minutes stirring them occasionally, then leave them to cool for a few minutes. Serve them hot in their syrup with a scoop of vanilla ice cream on top.

This is yummy served with thick slices of toasted Madeira cake and clotted or untreated cream. Just before serving, preheat the grill, cut about 6 slices of cake into fingers 2cm wide and lay them out on the rack of a grill pan. Grill the fingers on one side, watching carefully because once they start to colour they go very quickly. Turn and dust them with cinnamon and grill the second side too. You could replace half the redcurrants with blackcurrants, and use other berries as well as raspberries.

fruitcage compote

500g redcurrants
170g caster sugar
700g raspberries or
    loganberries
Madeira cake, toasted,
    to serve (optional)

Serves 6

String the redcurrants into a small pan using a fork, add the sugar and gently heat together for 4–5 minutes, stirring occasionally until the fruit is soft but still retains its shape, and is sitting in a pool of syrup. Place half the currants in a sieve and press their juice into a bowl and then return it to the pan, discarding the solids. Fold in the other berries, stir well and heat very gently for a minute or two, not to cook them but to encourage them to release their juices. Transfer the fruit to a serving bowl and leave to cool. Cover and chill if not serving in the near future, and bring the compote back up to room temperature half an hour before eating.

Don't be deterred by the word soup, this is still 100 per cent pudding. It's as cooling as an iced drink – a strawberry purée spiked with Cointreau with a few whole berries. It makes a graceful note on which to end, especially if you dress it up with lavender petals and cigarettes Russe.

strawberry soup

1.4kg strawberries, hulled
70g icing sugar
4 tablespoons Cointreau
  or Grand Marnier
Squeeze of lemon juice

To serve
Crème fraîche
Lavender petals (optional),
Toasted brioche or
  cigarettes Russes (optional)

Serves 6

Quarter 250g of the strawberries, cover and chill. Purée the remainder in a liquidiser with the icing sugar, liqueur and lemon juice. Pass the purée through a sieve, taste and add a little more sifted icing sugar if needed. Cover and chill for a couple of hours.

Divide the strawberry purée between six shallow soup bowls. Place a pile of the reserved strawberries in the centre, top with a teaspoon of crème fraîche, then scatter with lavender if you have any, and accompany with toasted brioche or cigarettes Russes.

Baking figs brings out the best in them: that lovely musky scent and succulence – and here amaretti provide a crispy crumble-like top. This is a genuine quickie: 5 minutes to assemble and 10 minutes to cook.

amaretti-stuffed figs

9 figs, stalks trimmed,
  and halved
80g soft amaretti
30g unsalted butter
30g light muscovado sugar
Crème fraîche or Greek yogurt
  to serve

Serves 4

Preheat the oven to 180°C fan/200°C/gas mark 6. Arrange the fig halves cut-side up in a baking dish with a little space in between. Whizz the amaretti, butter and sugar together in a food processor until the crumbs start to cling together into a crumble. Scatter this over the figs and bake for 10–15 minutes until golden.

To serve, I like them best hot or warm, with crème fraîche or Greek yogurt, though they're still good cold.

figs with mascarpone and saffron

Another lazy take is to spread about 6 halved figs with mascarpone and grill them. Blend 150g mascarpone with 30g icing sugar in a bowl, and if you like a little saffron liquor made from infusing strands in hot water. Spread over the cut side of each fig half, sprinkle with a little muscovado sugar and grill them for 4–5 minutes until golden and bubbling on top.

roast plums

The plums emerge from the oven in a pool of beautiful sticky deep purple juice, and are particularly good served with a raspberry sorbet. Remember to allow sorbet 20 minutes at room temperature before serving if it's frozen solid.

12 large juicy red plums,
  stalks removed
50g demerara sugar
4 tablespoons water
3 tablespoons Grand Marnier
  or Cointreau (or water)
Squeeze of lemon juice
10g unsalted butter, diced*

Serves 6

Preheat the oven to 180°C fan/200°C/gas mark 6. Place the whole plums in a shallow baking dish that will hold them snugly in a single layer. Scatter over the sugar and pour over the water and Grand Marnier or Cointreau. Roast for 25–30 minutes, basting halfway through. Transfer the plums to a bowl, sharpen the syrup with a generous squeeze of lemon juice and whisk in the butter. Pour the sauce over the fruit and serve with a dollop of raspberry sorbet if you have any.

*The plums are also delicious served at room temperature, in which case omit the butter.

Don't assume that mincemeat means Christmas; it contains everything that apples love – currants, raisins, lots of spices and citrus zest – and it's all there in a jar. You can serve these as they are, or with crème fraîche or clotted cream.

spicy baked apples

4 Bramley cooking apples,
   each about 220g
4 heaped tablespoons mincemeat
4 tablespoons maple syrup
2 tablespoons light muscovado sugar

Serves 4

Preheat the oven to 160°C fan/180°C/gas mark 4. Using the tip of a sharp knife, incise a circle around the middle of each apple, to allow them room to expand as they cook without the skin splitting. Cut out a central core from each apple about 4cm in diameter. Place the apples in a baking dish that holds them snugly side by side, and loosely stuff the core with the mincemeat. Drizzle over the syrup, and scatter the sugar over the top. Bake for 40–45 minutes, basting them halfway through.

Serve the apples 10–15 minutes out of the oven with the syrupy juices spooned over.

Luscious poached peaches in a rose-tinted syrup, flecked with black vanilla seeds. But as the recipe title suggests, quality is everything, only worth doing in mid-summer when you can be certain your peaches are dripping with juices.

peach perfect

6 ripe peaches
200ml dry white wine
1 vanilla pod, slit
100g caster sugar

Serves 6

Preheat the oven to 180°C fan/200°C/gas mark 6 and bring a large pan half filled with water to the boil. Dunk the peaches into the boiling water for 1 minute, then transfer them to a bowl or sink of cold water for a further minute or so, and slip off the skins.

Arrange the peaches in a shallow baking dish that holds them snugly, or with just a little space in between, and pour over the wine. Open out the vanilla pod and scrape out the seeds with a small sharp knife. Blend these with the sugar in a bowl and scatter over the peaches, then submerge the pod in the centre. Cover with foil and bake for 30 minutes, turning the peaches halfway through, and giving the syrup a gentle stir to help the sugar dissolve.

Transfer the peaches to a serving dish, pour over the syrup, leaving in the vanilla pod, and allow to cool. Cover and chill if not serving in the near future.

jellies

Jellies lie at the ethereal end of the dessert spectrum. Sparkling guilt-free gems, a playful palate-cleansing end to any feast. And after years of being relegated to children's parties they seem finally to be re-entering the adult arena of appreciation. They lend themselves to flavours as intense as their vibrant colours, in line with fruit pastilles or wine gums – strawberry, orange and blackberry – and those we can only wish for like pomegranate and watermelon. Almost anything else we prize by the small cup or glass is just as game: freshly brewed black coffee, rust-hued rooibos, and, the ultimate, Champagne or Prosecco – captured bubbles and all. If it tastes good to drink, then just think how delicious it'll taste once it's set.

The wide availability of leaf gelatine (see page 47) has made jellies more accessible. Once the sole preserve of chefs, leaf gelatine makes life very much easier; a mere glance at boiling water or liquid and it melts instantly. Powdered is a good second best, but steering it towards being fully dissolved is more challenging. It was a long time before I discovered the secret: to gently heat it in a small bowl set over a pan with a little simmering water in it as though melting chocolate. Dissolved this way there's no chance of it boiling, which is ruination to any set. But the texture is something you can play around with; be guided but not ruled by the packet instructions – you may prefer a light, almost creamy set that dissolves the minute you start eating it, or a firmer one if you are planning on turning out the jellies or using them as a showcase for other delights.

It's in the nature of a jelly to thrill, not least with its texture, but its appearance too. Setting fruits and other goodies into jelly is a trip back to the craft of making resin moulds. Instead of shells, leaves, stones and other such treasures, it's hidden fruits. The trick here is to leave your jelly to set in the fridge for about two hours, by which time it will have gelled enough to support any fruit you put into it without sinking. They're probably the prettiest of all puds too, either turned out or made in little glass bowls or dishes; there seems little point in hiding their light under a bushel.

Capturing bubbles in a jelly is a party trick that makes a great finale; the fizz is an amuse bouche in the true definition of the phrase, and creates a texture quite unlike any other jelly – almost crumbly. There's no need for anything on the side, except perhaps a few choccies to offset all that virtue, and some coffee to follow.

saffron and prosecco jelly

7 gelatine leaves (e.g. Supercook),
   cut into broad strips (or 1¾ sachets
   powdered gelatine, see page 47)
1 bottle prosecco, chilled
150g caster sugar
About 20 saffron filaments, ground

Serves 6

Place a 1 litre glass bowl (or six Champagne flutes if you have room) in the freezer for several hours or overnight. Place the gelatine strips in a bowl, cover with cold water and leave to soak for 5 minutes, then drain. Bring 100ml of the prosecco to the boil in a small pan with the sugar, stirring until it dissolves. Pour this over the saffron and blend, and then over the gelatine, again stirring until it dissolves.

Pour the gelatine solution into the chilled bowl, then gradually pour the rest of the bottle of prosecco over, constantly stirring to combine it with the gelatine. Spoon off any foam. Return the bowl to the freezer for 1 hour, then place it in the fridge for several hours longer or overnight until set.

A sparkling ruby red jelly, courtesy of a carton of juice that whisks you to the finishing line in minutes. This is a good one at any time of year, but dwell on it especially around Christmas, when pondering on a way of weaving these fruits into your celebrations.

pomegranate jelly

6 gelatine leaves
   (e.g. Supercook), cut into
   broad strips (or 1½ sachets
   powdered gelatine, see
   page 47)
150g strawberry jam
600ml pomegranate juice
Juice of ½ lemon
1 pomegranate, halved
Rose petals, to decorate
   (optional)

Rose cream (optional)
300ml whipping cream
50g icing sugar, sifted
2 teaspoons rosewater

Serves 6

Place the gelatine strips in a bowl, cover with cold water and leave to soak for 5 minutes, then drain.

Gently heat the jam in a small saucepan until it softens, mashing it with a spoon, then blend in a little of the pomegranate juice. Add the remainder, and the lemon juice, and heat until the liquid feels warm to the touch.

Pour a little of the juice over the soaked gelatine and stir until it dissolves. Stir the gelatine solution back into the juice and pass through a sieve into a serving bowl – it looks especially pretty in a glass one. Cover and chill overnight.

To serve, extract the pomegranate seeds by pressing down on the skin to pop them out, then pick out any white pith. Serve scattered over the jelly and decorate with rose petals if using.

To make the rose cream, whisk the whipping cream, sugar and rosewater in a bowl until it forms soft, fluffy peaks; I use an electric whisk. Cover and chill until required. If leaving it longer than a couple of hours, give it a stir and gently whisk with a spoon before serving with the jelly.

If you ever reach the point when you feel utterly replete after a lovely meal with friends, and the idea of getting up to make coffee casts a shadow over your peace but you feel the need to do the honourable, here is one way of circumventing the dilemma, and as it takes in pudding too you should be left feeling doubly relaxed.

black with cream

4 gelatine leaves (e.g. Supercook), cut into broad strips (or 1 sachet powdered gelatine, see page 47)
600ml freshly brewed filter coffee
100g golden caster sugar
2 tablespoons crème fraîche
Chocolate powder for dusting

Serves 6

Place the gelatine strips in a bowl, cover with cold water and leave to soak for 5 minutes, then drain.

Pour the coffee over the sugar in a jug or bowl and stir until it dissolves. Pour about half of this onto the soaked gelatine and stir until it melts, then stir the solution back into the coffee. Divide the solution between six small coffee cups or 150ml ramekins. Leave to cool, then cover and chill overnight until set (I put them in a roasting dish first). Serve the jellies with a teaspoon of crème fraîche and a dusting of chocolate powder.

As a child I longed to try watermelon after watching Goofy munching on a slice and spitting out the pips like a stream of gunfire. But I was disappointed when I got there, was the texture really worth all that trouble? Well, they've made life that much easier for today's children with the near absence of obvious pips in the majority of varieties, but that still leaves the texture. The flavour, though, is sublime, and a cool rose-pink jelly has to be the answer.

watermelon jelly

6 gelatine leaves (e.g. Supercook), cut into broad strips (or 1½ sachets powdered gelatine, see page 47)
900g watermelon flesh (trimmed weight), diced, large seeds removed
2 tablespoons lemon juice
180g caster sugar
300ml whipping cream, whipped
30g shelled pistachios, finely chopped or ground in a food processor

Serves 6

Place the gelatine strips in a bowl, cover with cold water and leave to soak for 5 minutes, then drain.

Place the watermelon in a liquidiser and reduce to a purée. Pass through a sieve into a measuring jug, and add the lemon juice. You should have about 800ml of liquid. Transfer this to a small saucepan and heat gently with the sugar until this dissolves; it should feel hot if you dip in your finger, without scalding. Add the soaked gelatine and stir until it dissolves.

Pour the solution into a glass serving dish (about 20 x 7cm deep), or six individual ones, leave to cool, then cover and chill for 2 hours until the jelly has just started to set. Give it a stir, then cover and chill overnight.

Shortly before serving, place a dollop of whipped cream on the jelly and scatter over the pistachios.

The 'really orange' is an intense hit of the fruit, achieved by simmering the juice to concentrate its flavour. It reminds me of that wonderful frozen orange juice that was the last word in luxury during my childhood. It came in cans and you diluted it with another can of juice, and it tasted just like sorbet if you managed to get in there when your mother wasn't looking. The chocolate custard is for chocolate-orange fiends, and is actually rather good on its own.

really orange jelly

Jelly
2 litres fresh orange juice, sieved
8 gelatine leaves (e.g. Supercook),
    cut into broad strips (or 2 sachets
    powdered gelatine, see page 47)
2 oranges
miniature chocolate orange segments
    or grated chocolate (optional)

Chocolate custard
400ml milk
4 medium organic egg yolks
90g milk chocolate (e.g. Lindt),
    broken into pieces
150g dark chocolate (50% cocoa),
    broken into pieces

Serves 6

Pour the orange juice into a large pan, bring to the boil and reduce by a third to 1.2 litres. If you over-do it, make up the volume with a little more orange juice.

Place the gelatine strips in a bowl, cover with cold water and leave to soak for 5 minutes, then drain. Pour a little of the reduced orange juice over the gelatine and stir until it dissolves, then add this back to the rest of the orange juice. Pour into a glass serving bowl and leave to cool.

Cut the skin and pith off the oranges, and run a sharp knife between the segments to remove them. Scatter these over the surface of the jelly – they should float. Cover and chill overnight. Serve the jelly with the chocolate custard on top, and if you like a chocolate orange segment or two. The jelly can be made several days in advance, in which case you can reduce the amount of gelatine to 6 leaves, as it will continue to set over a period of time.

To make the chocolate custard, bring the milk to the boil, whisk it onto the egg yolks, then pass through a sieve into a bowl. At the same time gently melt all the chocolate in a bowl set over a pan with a little simmering water in it. Whisk in the custard base, in four goes, until you have a rich chocolate cream. Cover and leave to cool, then chill for several hours or overnight.

I'm always on the lookout for ways of serving summer fruits beyond their usual remit of 'with cream', gorgeous though that is. This recipe has a clean and light edge, with the rasping hint of a little syrupy white wine in the way of gentle vice. The call for pretty small glass dishes or Champagne coupes is greater than ever.

summer jelly

3 gelatine leaves (e.g. Supercook),
 cut into broad strips (or
 ¾ sachet powdered gelatine,
 see page 47)
600ml Sauternes, or other
 sweet white wine
20g caster sugar
125g strawberries
50g blueberries
50g raspberries

Serves 4

Place the gelatine strips in a bowl, cover with cold water and leave to soak for 5 minutes, then drain.

Bring the wine and sugar to the boil in a small pan then immediately remove from the heat. Pour 3–4 tablespoons of the hot wine over the soaked gelatine and stir to dissolve, then add this back to the wine. Pour into four small glass bowls or glasses (allowing for the addition of fruit), or into one large one, cool, and then chill for 2–3 hours until the jelly is starting to set.

Hull the strawberries and halve if they are large. Fold all the fruit into the jelly, cover and leave to set overnight in the fridge.

whisked wine jelly

4 gelatine leaves (e.g. Supercook),
 cut into broad strips (or 1 sachet
 powdered gelatine, see page 47)
1 bottle Sauternes or other sweet
 white wine
40g caster sugar, or to taste

Serves 4–6

Place the gelatine strips in a bowl, cover with cold water and leave to soak for 5 minutes, then drain. Bring the wine to the boil in a pan and simmer for a couple of minutes, then remove from the heat. Add the sugar to taste, depending on the sweetness of the wine. Your jelly should be sweeter than you might want to drink the wine to counter the acidity of the fruit. Pour a little over the gelatine and stir until it dissolves, then add this back to the wine solution. Pour into a bowl and leave to cool, then cover and chill for 6 hours or overnight until it has set. To serve, run a whisk through it to break it up into a soft chopped mass and spoon it over whatever fruits you are serving (choose from stoned cherries, sliced peaches, raspberries, loganberries and strawberries).

When Jo Malone launched her wonderful esoteric perfume range, it was an inspiration in how scents were created. The way she subtly employed fruits and spices to lift other notes was the starting point for this jelly, as mysterious as it is dark. A prize for anyone who guesses the tea that so naturally flows as an undercurrent to the blackberry.

blackberry and tea jelly

3 gelatine leaves (e.g. Supercook), cut into broad strips
(or ¾ sachet powdered gelatine, see page 47)
75g caster sugar
400ml hot Earl Grey tea
350g blackberries
Silver balls (optional)

Serves 6

Place the gelatine strips in a bowl, cover with cold water and leave to soak for 5 minutes, then drain.

Add the sugar to the hot tea in a jug or bowl and stir until it dissolves. Pour about half of this onto the soaked gelatine and stir until it melts, then stir the solution back into the tea. Set aside 6 juicy blackberries for decoration, and purée the rest in a liquidiser. Pass the purée through a sieve, and stir it into the tea. Pour the solution into six 150ml ramekins or small glasses. Leave to cool, then cover and chill overnight until set (I put them in a roasting dish first).

Serve each jelly with a blackberry in the centre and a few silver balls for added glitz if wished.

Also known as Red Bush, we have latched on to this rust-coloured tea that grows wild in South Africa, not least because it sings with anti-oxidants and has the greatest anti-ageing properties of any plant in the world. You can't ask much more than that from a pudding.

rooibos jelly

3 gelatine leaves (e.g. Supercook),
   cut into broad strips (or ¾ sachet
   powdered gelatine, see page 47)
120g caster sugar
3 tablespoons rooibos tea
Juice of 1 orange
1 tablespoon lemon juice
2 passionfruit, halved

Serves 4

Place the gelatine strips in a bowl, cover with cold water and leave to soak for 5 minutes, then drain.

Place the sugar in a measuring jug, fill up to 500ml with boiling water and stir to dissolve. Pour this over the tea in another jug or medium-size bowl, give it a stir and leave to infuse for 5 minutes. Strain the tea through a fine-mesh sieve or tea-strainer over the gelatine and stir to dissolve. Add the orange and lemon juice and strain through a sieve a second time, into a jug or bowl.

Rinse four 150ml ramekins or small glasses. Pour the jelly solution into them and leave to cool. Cover with clingfilm (I put them in a roasting dish first), then place in the fridge to set overnight.

To serve, either smooth the passionfruit seeds over the top of each jelly and serve from the dish, or briefly dip the moulds into a bowl of boiling water, run a knife around the edge and turn out onto plates. Spoon the seeds over and around.

This is kiddie heaven, something like a glorious fruit pastille that's rather bigger than usual. In fact it almost gets thumbs up over the packet strawberry jelly, those concentrated pull-off squares that vie for supremacy with 'blackcurrant and glycerine' cough pastilles as contraband sweeties.

strawberry jellies

3 gelatine leaves (e.g. Supercook),
    cut into broad strips or ¾ sachet
    powdered gelatine, see page 47)
900g strawberries
100g golden caster sugar
Juice of 1 lemon
Clotted cream (optional)

Serves 4

Place the gelatine strips in a bowl, cover with cold water and soak for 5 minutes, then drain.

Set aside 4 small strawberries for decoration and hull the remainder, cutting up large ones. Purée these in a liquidiser with the sugar and lemon juice, then pass the purée through a sieve into a small pan. Bring to the boil, then pour it into a measuring jug, you should have about 600ml of liquid (make up the amount with water if need be).

Pour a little of this over the soaked gelatine and stir to dissolve, then stir in the remainder. Divide the jelly solution between four 150ml ramekins or other little pots and leave to cool. Cover and chill overnight. Serve decorated with a strawberry in the middle, with a spoon of clotted cream if wished.

Campari with lemon is an acquired taste for those with a penchant for a little sophisticated bitterness in their life, but try this jelly and it's easy to see why they're thrown together: good friends that reveal each other's hidden charms.

campari and lemon jellies with passionfruit

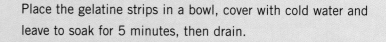

4 gelatine leaves
(e.g. Supercook),
cut into broad strips
(or 1 sachet
powdered gelatine,
see page 47)

180g caster sugar
Juice of 3 lemons
2 tablespoons Campari
3 passionfruit, halved

Serves 6

Place the gelatine strips in a bowl, cover with cold water and leave to soak for 5 minutes, then drain.

Place the sugar in a measuring jug and fill up to 300ml with boiling water and stir to dissolve. Pour a little of this over the gelatine and stir to dissolve, then add this back to the solution. Now add the lemon juice and the Campari and make up to 600ml with boiling water. Strain through a sieve into six rinsed 150ml ramekins or other little pots. Cover with clingfilm (I place them in a roasting dish for this), leave to cool and then place in the fridge to set overnight.

To serve, briefly dip the moulds into a bowl of boiling water, run a knife around the edge and turn out onto plates. Spoon the seeds from half a passionfruit over each one.

gelatine

the set

The amount of gelatine used can be varied depending on the type of set you want. If you are planning on turning the jelly out, add a little bit extra. Equally, if you like your jellies on the wobbly side you can use a little less. It's always worth bearing in mind that the jelly will continue to set over a period of days, so if you are making it well in advance, then you can reduce the quantity slightly.

leaf gelatine

Leaf gelatine is now widely available and dissolves more readily than powdered. However, brands do tend to differ, and not all of them give accurate recommendations for quantities. All these jellies have been tested using Supercook leaf gelatine, 4 leaves will set 600ml liquid.

To use the leaf form, cut the gelatine into broad strips, place in a bowl, cover with cold water and leave to soak for 5 minutes, then drain it.

powdered gelatine

This comes in sachets of a standard weight of 12g that sets 600ml liquid, again Supercook can be relied on. Sprinkle the gelatine over a few tablespoons of just-boiled water in a small bowl, as opposed to the other way around. Leave it for 3–4 minutes to soften, then stir for a minute or two, by which time you should have a clear sticky solution.

problem solving

If the gelatine hasn't completely dissolved, place the bowl within another bowl of just-boiled water and leave for a few minutes longer, then give it a good stir. Alternatively, pour the mixture into a bowl set over a pan with a little simmering water in it, as though you were melting chocolate, and gently heat. It's essential the gelatine solution is never actually boiled, as this will destroy its ability to set.

adding the gelatine

Ideally add the gelatine solution to a warm base, diluting the molten gelatine with a little warmed liquid first. You can then incorporate it with the rest of the warm jelly base.

If you add gelatine solution to a cold liquid it will immediately set into rubbery lumps. There is a way around this, however. If the base of the jelly is cold, very gradually whisk the cold solution into the gelatine solution, or add about 8 tablespoons of the base, one at a time, and then add this back to the base.

ice cool

This chapter is welcome to everyone, with or without an ice-cream maker. You can easily make delectable frozen desserts in their absence that will top anything made in a machine. And with the help of a food processor, you again don't need one. If you half-freeze a mixture, whizz it to a slush and then continue to freeze it, you will still produce a fine homemade ice cream. And if this seems like too much work, you can have some fun running up wildly extravagant ice cream bombes and layered terrines using tubs of ready-made and a few other bits and bobs. Let your mind wander to that small square in Italy where you sheltered from the midday sun and chose ices off a picture menu...

I cannot resist the great classic ice creams: a really dense fudgey chocolate or a silky vanilla flecked with the black of vanilla seeds that can be conjured into a Peach Melba with raspberry sauce and slivers of peach, and of course that English eccentric: brown bread ice cream – a mass of caramelised breadcrumbs folded into cream and frozen. But when I'm after something truly simple, then it's a shot of bitter espresso coffee poured over a scoop of vanilla.

I sometimes favour sorbets over ice creams at the end of dinner as they round off an occasion in more palate-cleansing fashion, providing the same sparkle as fresh jellies and fruit. For me, sorbets flavoured with deep-hued juices like strawberry and blackcurrant hit the spot: there's something irresistible about a mass of miniscule dark vermilion ice crystals that dye your tongue and lips red or dramatically purple. And while they're delicious eaten within a few hours of being churned, they can also be revived after a week or so – unlike ice creams. Simply leave them to melt, then add a little hooch or some other conceit should the flavour need enlivening and rechurn the mixture.

The gin makes a nice jazzy touch, and calls up hidden memories of English gardens and lunches. But if you're making this with kiddies in mind, nothing will seem amiss should you leave it out, though they might appreciate some iced gems scattered over.

strawberry and gin sorbet

250ml boiling water
250g caster sugar
800g strawberries, hulled
Juice of 1 lemon
4 tablespoons gin
Cornets to serve

Serves 8

Pour the boiling water over the sugar in a bowl, stir until it dissolves and leave to cool. Purée the strawberries, lemon juice and gin in a blender and pass through a sieve. Combine the strawberry purée with the syrup, and freeze according to the instructions for your ice-cream maker. It is less stressful on the motor if you chill the solution first. Scoop the sorbet into a container, seal and freeze for several hours or overnight.

Alternatively, pour the mixture into a plastic container, seal it and freeze for 2–3 hours until it is half-frozen, hard around the outside and soft within, but start checking it after 1 hour. Scoop it into a food processor and whizz to break up the ice-crystals, at which point it will be like a thick slush. Return it to the container and freeze for a further 2 hours until you have a soft but firm sorbet. If leaving it longer than this and it has frozen solid, it may need 15–30 minutes out of the freezer to return to the right consistency.

Serve in cornets to go.

This one takes the title ice cream rather literally, consisting quite simply of crushed raspberries, clotted cream and icing sugar, chilled down and down. It's designed to be eaten as soon as it's churned, or at least within an hour of being frozen.

raspberry and clotted cream ice

450g raspberries
350g clotted cream
150g icing sugar, sifted
Cantuccini to serve (optional)

Serves 6

Place the raspberries in the bowl of a food processor and briefly whizz to reduce to a textured purée. Beat the cream and sugar in a large bowl until smooth, then fold in the raspberries in two goes. You can make this in advance and freeze it shortly before serving, in which case cover and chill it at this stage.

Freeze the raspberries and cream mixture according to the instructions for your ice-cream maker. Ideally serve the ice immediately, but it will keep in the fridge for up to an hour. Serve with cantuccini if liked.

This blackcurrant sorbet is the most intensely flavoured ice I know, matched by its Renaissance hue of deep purple. In essence it's everything you love about a Kir Royale, in a sophisticated ice-cream parlour fashion.

kir float

500g blackcurrants, fresh, or frozen
  and defrosted
150g golden caster sugar
150ml water
1 bottle chilled Champagne

Serves 6

Place the blackcurrants in a medium pan with the sugar and water. Bring to the boil, then cover and cook over a low heat for 5 minutes. Press the mixture through a sieve over a bowl to collect the thick deep-purple syrup. Leave this to cool, then cover and chill for a couple of hours.

If you have an ice-cream maker then freeze according to the instructions. Scoop the sorbet into a container, seal and freeze for at least 4 hours or overnight.

Alternatively, transfer the mixture to a shallow container, cover or seal it and freeze for about 2 hours until the mixture is half-frozen, hard around the outside and soft within, but start checking it after 1 hour. Scoop it into a food processor and whizz to a thick slush to break up the ice crystals. Return the sorbet to the container and freeze for a further 4 hours or overnight.

Depending on how hard the sorbet has frozen, it may need about 20 minutes out of the freezer. Place a scoop of sorbet in the bottom of six glasses and fill up with Champagne.

If you had to have just one classic on the menu, a promise of instant cooling palate-cleansing refreshment, then this would have to be it. And OK you can scoop out some lemons and fill them.

lemon sorbet

375ml boiling water
250g caster sugar (refined)
5 lemons

Serves 4

Pour the boiling water over the sugar in a bowl and stir until dissolved. Remove the zest from 3 of the lemons using a potato peeler, add to the syrup and leave to cool completely for about an hour. Add the juice from the lemons to the syrup, and pass through a sieve. Cover and chill the solution for several hours or overnight.

If using an ice-cream maker, freeze according to the instructions, then scoop the sorbet into a container or into lemon shells, seal and freeze for several hours or overnight.

Alternatively pour the solution into a container, seal and freeze until softly frozen, start checking it after about 3 hours, and hourly thereafter. Scoop the sorbet into the bowl of a food processor and whizz to a slush, then return it to the freezer (or scoop into lemon shells) for another few hours or overnight.

If the sorbet has frozen very hard, then you may need to remove it about 20 minutes before serving.

Every cook needs a really good, rich chocolate ice cream up their sleeve, and this one challenges Häagen-Dazs® for supremacy, who famously set theirs with chocolate chips, which might be worth trying too.

really chocolatey semifreddo

100g dark chocolate (70% cocoa),
    broken into pieces
300ml double cream
3 organic eggs, separated
150g icing sugar
½ teaspoon vanilla extract
white chocolate shavings to serve

Serves 6

Gently melt the chocolate in a bowl set over a pan with a little simmering water in it. Bring the cream to the boil in a small non-stick pan. Whisk the egg yolks and half of the sugar together in a bowl, then gradually whisk in the hot cream, it should thicken into a thin custard instantly. Pass it through a sieve into a bowl, then whisk it into the melted chocolate in about three goes, and stir in the vanilla. Cover the surface with clingfilm and leave to cool to room temperature.

Whisk the egg whites until stiff, then gradually sprinkle over the remaining sugar a tablespoon at a time, whisking well with each addition until you have a stiff glossy meringue; I use a hand-held electric whisk. Fold the egg whites into the cooled chocolate custard in two goes. Line a 1.1 litre pudding basin or plastic container with clingfilm and pour in the mixture, then cover the surface with clingfilm and freeze overnight. The ice cream can also be made in a plastic container.

If making it in a pudding basin as a bombe, dip the bowl into a sink of hot water to loosen the ice cream, then turn it out onto a plate and remove the clingfilm. Leave to soften for about 10 minutes, then scatter with chocolate shavings. Otherwise remove from the freezer about 20 minutes before eating, and serve in scoops with the chocolate shavings scattered over.

This is the one we all keep coming back to, the great foundation, and it has to be the consistency of liquid velvet and flecked with vanilla seeds. But my first excursion would be a peach melba, come the summertime. Plunge ripe peaches into boiling water for a minute and then into cold water and peel off their skins. Serve a peach half with a scoop of vanilla and trickles of fresh raspberry sauce for one of the most elegant trios you can conjure up.

vanilla ice with raspberry sauce

Ice cream
200g golden caster sugar
Zest of 1 lemon, removed
   with a potato peeler
300ml water
1 vanilla pod, slit
450ml double cream
9 medium organic egg yolks

Raspberry sauce
450g raspberries
75g icing sugar
1 tablespoon lemon juice

Serves 6

Place the sugar and lemon zest in a small pan with the water. Open out the vanilla pod and scrape out the seeds with a small sharp knife. Add these to the pan with the pod. Bring to the boil over a medium-high heat and cook for 15–25 minutes until you have a thick syrup, it should register 115°C or 'soft ball' on a jam thermometer. Meanwhile, whisk the cream in a large bowl until stiff.

Discard the lemon zest and vanilla pod, drizzle the syrup onto the egg yolks in a food processor with the motor running. Continue to whizz for a couple of minutes until the mixture turns pale and creamy, then transfer it to a large mixing bowl and stir for a minute or so until it cools to room temperature.

Whisk the cream into the egg yolk and sugar mixture in two goes, then transfer it to a container, seal and freeze overnight.

To make the sauce, place the raspberries, icing sugar and lemon juice in a liquidiser and whizz to a purée. Pass through a sieve, then cover and chill until required.

Remove the ice cream from the freezer about 20 minutes before eating. Serve with the raspberry sauce.

As a child I wanted to emigrate to America, the land where you get marshmallows in cereal, so this version of brown bread ice cream has a certain transatlantic appeal for me. Though they're not essential.

brown bread and marshmallow ice cream

75g fresh brown breadcrumbs
75g light muscovado sugar
3 medium organic egg whites
50g icing sugar

300ml double cream
100g mini marshmallows

Serves 6–8

Preheat the oven to 180°C fan/200°C/gas mark 6. Whizz together the breadcrumbs and muscovado sugar in the bowl of a food processor, then spread the mixture out in a thin layer on a baking tray. Toast for 6–8 minutes until the crumbs are turning golden around the outside. Scrape them into the centre and spread them out again, and toast for a further 2–3 minutes until evenly gold, then leave to cool for a few minutes.

Whisk the egg whites until they have risen, then sprinkle over the icing sugar, a tablespoon at a time, whisking well with each addition, until you have a stiff glossy meringue. In a separate bowl, whip the cream to stiff peaks.

Run a rolling pin over the crumbs to break them up. Fold the egg whites into the cream, then the crumbs and the marshmallows. Transfer the mixture to a container, seal and freeze overnight. Remove 20–25 minutes before eating.

The form here is to pour
scalding bitter espresso
over a scoop of frozen solid
vanilla ice, then start to
work the coffee into the
melted edges and eat it
spoon by spoon as it
softens to a creamy tan-
coloured ice. Like the Black
with Cream on page 35,
it's one of those puddings
that rounds off a delicious
lunch or dinner when you
feel like something sweet
without going the whole
hog of a rich dessert.

affogato al caffe

4 scoops vanilla ice cream,
  frozen solid
4 shots of freshly brewed
  espresso coffee

Serves 4

Whereas normally you need to soften ice cream straight from the freezer before
serving it, here it should be frozen rock hard. If you are using homemade ice
cream (see page 60), churn and freeze it overnight.

Place four scoops of ice cream in four small bowls or cups. Trickle a shot of
freshly brewed espresso over each one and serve.

It's those cherry red lips and buttermilk skin that call up this bombe's namesake. This is the easiest possible pud, you simply have to attend to it in stages, but even then if you forget and leave it in the freezer longer than the specified time, it won't come to any harm.

snow white bombe

2 x 500ml tubs vanilla ice cream
150g black cherry jam (e.g. St Dalfour)
1½ tablespoons brandy
Generous squeeze of lemon juice
Amaretti to serve (optional)

Serves 6

Remove one of the tubs of ice cream from the freezer and leave it to soften for about 20 minutes. Scoop this into a litre pudding bowl or other similar deep dish, and use to line the base and sides, leaving a well in the centre. Cover the surface with clingfilm and freeze for 2 hours until it firms up.

Work the jam in a bowl to loosen it, then blend in the brandy and lemon juice. Fill the cavity of the ice cream bombe – you may have to excavate the hollow again if it has filled itself in. Cover and freeze for a further couple of hours.

Remove the second tub of ice cream from the freezer, again leave to soften for about 20 minutes, and then fill the pudding bowl to the top and smooth the surface (you will have a little left over in the tub). Cover and freeze overnight.

Remove from the freezer about 20 minutes before serving. Dip the bowl into a sink of hot water, then run a knife around the edge of the bombe and turn it out onto a plate. Serve in slices, with some amaretti if wished.

This is a Sixties-Seventies thing – you may or may not remember those blocks of layered ice cream; perhaps you were too young. This ice-cream cake has the hidden surprise of a layer of meringue and jam in the middle. Any summery flavour can be partnered with the chocolate: raspberry, strawberry, peach, cherry ... whatever other delightful hot-weather flavours the freezer cabinet is offering up. Pistachio is particularly good if you can get it.

neo-politan pavlova ice

1 x 500ml tub chocolate ice cream
1 x 500ml tub pistachio or other ice
  cream of contrasting colour
75g raspberry or strawberry jam
3 meringue nests, finely crumbled

Serves 8

Remove the chocolate ice cream from the freezer 30–45 minutes in advance, so that it's really soft. Smooth the chocolate ice cream over the base of a 22cm (1.3 litre) loaf or terrine tin, pressing it into the corners and levelling the surface. Wipe any smudges around the edge with kitchen paper, then cover the surface with clingfilm and freeze for a couple of hours.

Remove the pistachio ice cream from the freezer 30–45 minutes in advance. Gently heat the jam in a small pan until it loosens, then press it through a sieve. It should be at room temperature, so if necessary leave it to cool. Smooth a third of the ice cream over the chocolate ice cream, scatter over the crumbled meringue and gently press it down, drizzle over the jam then smooth over the rest of the ice cream, again pressing it down and smoothing the surface. Cover the surface with clingfilm and freeze for at least 4 hours, or overnight.

To serve, briefly dip the terrine in a sink of hot water, run a knife around the edge, turn it out onto a plate or board and cut into slices.

Were you an actress trying to pile on the pounds for a new part, sitting around dipping into a tub of ice cream would do the trick in no time at all. Which, given how close it is to a girl's heart, makes it something of a problem. The Indians seem to have got it just right with kulfi, not as austere as a sorbet, it relies on milk that is reduced to enrich it.

pistachio kulfi

1.8 litres full-cream milk
1 level teaspoon cornflour
150g caster sugar
1 tablespoon rosewater
70g shelled pistachios,

Serves 6

Pour the milk into a large pan, bring to the boil and simmer for about 45 minutes over a medium heat to reduce by half. Don't worry about the skin that forms during the process of cooking, simply lift this off at the end. Blend 1 tablespoon of the reduced milk with the cornflour, return it to the saucepan and simmer for several minutes until it thickens a little. Remove from the heat, add the sugar and stir to dissolve, then add the rosewater. Pour through a sieve into a jug or bowl, cover the surface with clingfilm and leave to cool. Chill for a couple of hours or overnight.

Grind 50g of the pistachios to a powder in an electric coffee grinder and finely chop the remaining 20g. Stir the ground pistachios into the ice-cream base, and then the chopped ones.

Freeze the mixture according to the instructions for your ice-cream maker. Either serve it immediately, or transfer it to a plastic container, cover and freeze. It is at its best eaten within about 3 hours, if keeping it any longer then remove from the freezer 30 minutes before serving to allow it to soften a little.

Alternatively pour the solution into a container, seal and freeze until softly frozen, start checking it after about 2 hours, and hourly thereafter. Scoop the ice into the bowl of a food processor and whizz to a slush, then return it to the freezer for another few hours.

These little cakes are delicious eaten with ices and sorbets (or a fruit dessert, see page 13). You can either make them in boat or scallop shapes if your cake-tin cupboard runs to these, or little fairy-cake moulds, or 'bun racks' as they are now known.

sultana madeleines

2 large eggs
25g caster sugar
Finely grated zest of 1 lemon
2 tablespoons clear honey
50g plain flour
1 teaspoon baking powder
50g ground almonds
125g unsalted butter, melted
50g sultanas
Icing sugar for dusting

Makes 12–15

Whisk the eggs and sugar together in a bowl until they are almost white. Add the lemon zest and the honey. Sift the flour and baking powder together into a bowl, then lightly fold into the honey mixture with the ground almonds. Brush the insides of the cake tins with a little of the melted butter and fold the remainder into the cake mixture. Cover and chill for 30 minutes.

Meanwhile preheat the oven to 190°C fan/210°C/gas mark 6. Fold the sultanas into the cake mixture and fill the moulds by two-thirds. Bake for 9–10 minutes until golden.

Run a knife around the edge of the cakes to loosen them and turn them out onto a wire rack to cool. Dust with icing sugar at the last minute and arrange on a plate. While they are nicest eaten barely cooled, you can store them in an airtight container for a couple of days.

This is a classic sorbet sugar syrup that can also be used for poaching fruits or sweetening fruit sauces. It keeps well in the fridge for up to 2 weeks.

sugar syrup

300g caster sugar
300ml boiling water

Makes 425ml

Place the sugar in a bowl, pour the boiling water over and stir until the sugar dissolves. Leave the syrup to cool to room temperature then cover and chill it until required.

It's worth remembering to chill your sorbet mixture before churning to save overworking your ice-cream maker, as some of them are more efficient than others.

the perfect consistency

Most homemade ice cream needs to be removed from the freezer a little way in advance to ensure it has that soft melting consistency. But how long will depend on the type of ice cream and whether it's resided in an ice-box at the top of the fridge or in a deep-freeze. A quick prod should tell you more or less how long it needs. For just that little bit of softening then 10–15 minutes should do it; if it's rock hard then closer to 30 minutes before serving.

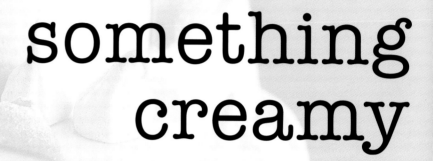

something creamy

Given our historic love of ice cream it's not hard to see why that extends to other creamy silken puds, especially when they come in little pots or glasses. I wonder if we don't sometimes try to fool ourselves that these miniatures are mere will-o'-the-wisps, hardly even counting as pudding. So small in fact many of us find room for another, and another little pot of something creamy.

Top pot has to be a competition between crème brûlée and crème caramel, though increasingly my vote goes to the latter, cooling and lightly set, its glassy surface dyed gold with caramel that dissolves into a sauce around it. And it's foolproof, the caramel is guaranteed, unlike a crème brûlée. Mainly due to a reluctance to own a mini blow torch, I usually try to find other ways of finishing this delectable cream, whether it's with a jammy fruit compote spread on top, or by flavouring the cream with coffee and scattering over some grated chocolate.

Fluffy fruit fools also lie close to our heart, anything tart and intense is game, rhubarb makes a particularly spendid fool, and raspberries too are as sour as they are sweet, and that allows for the introduction of lots of cream. Anything untreated will have that much more to offer than a pasteurised cream, aim for something thick and yellow.

But if ever we needed proof that what goes around comes around, and that all food fashions of value reappear at some point, then we have only to look to the recent reinstatement of Marie Antoinette as a French national heroine, and with it the makeover of blancmange. Finally rescued from a corner of the nursery and reborn as deliciously decadent and sexy. Towering pastel-hued custards, an acquired taste perhaps, but they are back and those of you who have given cupboard space to that large copper jelly mould for so long now will finally be vindicated.

I bet a surprising number of us have aunty's Victorian jelly or blancmange mould squirrelled away in the attic, the tiered curvilinear form of la belle époque that we couldn't bear to part with, so dust it off as it's about to come into its own. You can embellish this blancmange with sugared almonds – pink, white and silver all work a treat. Then think of the vibrant pastel shades of Ladurée's macaroons, deep yellow-hued lemon and the dark pink of mixed red fruits.

raspberry blancmange

Groundnut or vegetable
 oil for brushing
3 gelatine leaves (e.g. Supercook),
 cut into broad strips (or ¾ sachet
 powdered gelatine, see page 47)
400g raspberries
125g icing sugar
300ml double cream

To serve
Macaroons
Sugared almonds

Serves 6

Lightly brush a 600ml jelly mould with oil. Place the gelatine strips in a bowl, cover with cold water and leave to soak for 5 minutes, then drain.

Whizz the raspberries and sugar together in a liquidiser, then press the purée through a sieve. Gently heat the cream in a small pan until it feels hot to the touch. Add the gelatine and stir until it dissolves, then stir in the raspberry purée. Pour the cream into the mould, cover and chill overnight.

To turn out the blancmange, briefly dip the mould into a sink of hot water and run a knife around the top. Place a plate or board over the mould and invert it, gently easing the blancmange out. This can be done in advance, in which case cover and chill it until required.

Shortly before serving, decorate with macaroons and sugared almonds.

There's a small group of fruits that you only have to conjure in your mind for your mouth to start watering. Rhubarb, gooseberries, redcurrants and lemons come alive as soon as you challenge their sourness with an equally large dose of sugar, and even better the same amount of cream. My heart sinks when I come across gooseberry and rhubarb sauces to serve with salmon and other savoury dishes; I can see the rationale but it never quite works in the way that a fool does, which is home for both fruits. You can make the fool up to 24 hours in advance. The biscuits are a little added extra, yummy with any creamy little pud.

rhubarb fool

Fool

500g rhubarb, trimmed
   and cut into 2cm lengths
125g golden caster sugar
500ml whipping cream
2 tablespoons Cointreau

Serves 6

Poppyseed biscuits

75g plain flour
25g golden caster sugar
60g unsalted butter, diced
Pinch of sea salt
½ tablespoon poppyseeds
1 medium egg yolk
Vegetable oil for greasing

Makes 15–20

Place the rhubarb in a medium pan with the sugar, cover and gently heat for 10 minutes, stirring it halfway through, until it has softened and given out its juices. Simmer uncovered for a further 20–30 minutes until you have a thick, dry purée, stirring occasionally especially towards the end to make sure it doesn't stick. Transfer the rhubarb to a large bowl and leave to cool.

Whisk the cream with the Cointreau in a large bowl until stiff; I use an electric hand-held whisk. Fold it into the rhubarb purée in three goes to give a marbled effect and transfer to a large serving bowl, glasses or individual dishes, cover and chill until required.

To make the biscuits, put the flour, sugar, butter, salt and poppyseeds in the bowl of a food processor and reduce to crumbs. Add the egg yolk and bring the dough together into a ball. Wrap in clingfilm and chill for 1 hour.

Preheat the oven to 180°C fan/200°C/gas mark 5 and oil a baking tray. Knead the dough until pliable, then thinly roll it out on a lightly floured surface, about 2mm thick. Cut out biscuits using a 5cm round biscuit cutter, rolling the dough twice, and lay these 1cm apart on the baking tray. Bake for 9–12 minutes until a pale gold, then remove and leave the biscuits to cool on the tray. Transfer them to a plate using a palette knife. They will keep well in a covered container for several days.

Travel back to the court at Versailles and the way powdered and jewelled young ladies broke into those tiered blancmanges using their fingers, at least on celluloid, which I've always fancied doing if never had the occasion to. For the full fantasy, buy up the sugared roses, the ribbon, the baby meringues, and put your vintage brocade shoes on.

rose folly

12 gelatine leaves (e.g. Supercook),
  cut into broad strips (or 3 sachets
  powdered gelatine, see page 47)
600ml milk
3 tablespoons rosewater
200g caster sugar (refined)
Zest of 1 lemon, removed with a
  potato peeler
600ml whipping cream
Pink or peach food colouring liquid
  or paste

To serve
Baby meringues
Crystallised rose petals or sugar roses

Serves 8

Place the gelatine strips in a bowl, cover with cold water and soak for 5 minutes, then drain. Bring the milk, rosewater, sugar and lemon zest to the boil, stirring until the sugar dissolves. Remove from the heat, add the gelatine and stir until it dissolves, then leave to cool for about 1 hour to room temperature.

Strain the cooled milk. Whisk the cream in a large bowl until stiff; I use a hand-held electric whisk, then gradually whisk in the milk, and colour the mixture a pastel shade of pink or peach with a very little food colour.

Lightly brush a 20cm soufflé dish with oil, and four 150ml ramekins. Fill the ramekins, and pour the remaining cream mixture into the soufflé dish. Cover and chill overnight.

To assemble the blancmange, briefly dip the soufflé dish into a sink of hot water, run a knife around the edge, place a plate or board over the mould and invert it. Next run a knife around the edge of each ramekin, and ease the blancmange out, arranging 3 of them in a triangle on top of the large blancmange. Place the fourth on top in the centre, so that you have three tiered layers. This can be done an hour or two in advance, in which case cover and chill the assembly.

Just before serving, decorate with baby meringues, and crystallised rose petals or sugar roses.

A silky rose-scented mousse scattered with pistachios and every bit as luxurious as a fine ice cream. I suppose anything that's pale pink and perfumed comes with its fair share of girl appeal, though you can always forego the colour.

chilled rose soufflés

2 gelatine leaves (e.g. Supercook),
   cut into broad strips (or ½ sachet
   powdered gelatine, see page 47)
180ml milk
5 medium egg yolks
125g caster sugar

1 tablespoon rosewater
Pink or red food colouring liquid or
   paste (optional)
300ml whipping cream
2 tablespoons finely chopped pistachios

Serves 6

Place the gelatine strips in a bowl, cover with cold water and leave to soak for 5 minutes, then drain.

Bring the milk to the boil in a small non-stick pan. Whisk the egg yolks and sugar together in a bowl, then whisk in the milk. Return the mixture to the pan and cook over a low heat, stirring almost constantly until the mixture thickens into a thin custard that coats the back of a spoon. Pass through a sieve onto the gelatine and stir to dissolve, then stir in the rosewater. If you like you can also colour it pink with a little food colouring. Cover the surface with clingfilm and leave to cool completely, about 1 hour.

Use an electric whisk to stiffly whip the cream in a large bowl, then fold in the cooled custard in two goes. Divide the mousse between six 150ml ramekins or other little bowls or cups. Place the dishes in a roasting dish or on a small tray, cover with clingfilm and chill overnight until set. Shortly before serving scatter some pistachios in the centre.

I always associate this one with moules marinières: going back many years we always served this to follow. It's the stuff of relaxed kitchen suppers with just a handful of friends or family who won't mind if you retreat into a deep concentration at the stove and keep them waiting for ten minutes before it's ready. It's always worth waiting for.

zabaglione

4 medium organic egg yolks
50g golden caster sugar
100ml Marsala

Serves 6

Whisk together the egg yolks and sugar in a largish bowl that will allow for the zabaglione to swell into a foamy mass. Set the bowl over a pan with a little simmering water in it, add the Marsala and using a hand-held electric whisk (you can do this with an ordinary whisk but it will take much longer), start whisking the mixture on a medium speed. It will rise and become frothy relatively quickly, but continue to whisk the mixture until it is the consistency of whipped cream. This will take about 5–8 minutes. Remove the bowl from the heat and serve.

Unlike a souffle zabaglione doesn't sink instantly when removed from the heat, and will stand around for a few minutes.

A mixing of cultures here, panna cotta can only benefit from the added flavour of a little Gallic crème fraîche over normal cream. These puds are rich by design, and wallow in a shot of eau-de-vie, tempered by the sharp burst of redcurrants.

panna cotta with redcurrants

2 gelatine leaves (e.g. Supercook), cut into broad strips (or ½ sachet of powdered gelatine, see page 47)
450g crème fraîche
75g caster sugar
1 vanilla pod, slit
4 tablespoons kirsch or other fruit eau-de-vie
8 sprigs of redcurrants

Serves 4

Place the gelatine strips in a bowl, cover with cold water and soak for 5 minutes, then drain. Pour a few tablespoons of boiling water over the gelatine and stir until it dissolves.

Place the crème fraîche and sugar in a small pan and gently heat until the cream melts and the sugar dissolves, then remove from the heat. Open out the vanilla pod and scrape out the seeds with a small sharp knife. Blend a little of the crème fraîche with the seeds and blend this back into the rest of the cream in the saucepan.

Stir a little of the cream into the gelatine, and then return this to the rest of the cream. Pour the mixture into four small glasses or 150ml ramekin dishes. Cover and chill in the fridge for several hours or overnight until set.

To serve, run a knife around the edge of each cream to loosen it, and then turn it out onto a plate. Pour a tablespoon of eau-de-vie over each cream. String the redcurrant sprigs and scatter around the sides of each panna cotta, or drape one redcurrant sprig on top of each serving.

The thin layer of caramel on top of a crème brûlée that invites us to dip in our spoons is all but impossible to achieve without a small blowtorch, which is one piece of kitchen equipment most of us can live without, given its occasional use. I prefer to make the caramel in a saucepan and drizzle just a little over, it looks even prettier and you still get that burnt sugar crunch.

crème brûlée

Cream

6 medium egg yolks

3 heaped tablespoons caster sugar

1 vanilla pod, chopped

600ml double cream

Icing sugar for dusting

Caramel

125g caster sugar

Serves 6

Preheat the oven to 140°C fan/160°C/gas mark 3. Whizz all the ingredients for the cream together in a blender, and pass through a sieve into a bowl or jug. Divide between six 150ml ramekins and place them in a roasting dish with hot but not boiling water that comes two-thirds of the way up the sides. Bake for 60–75 minutes until lightly golden on the surface. They should be set but may gently wobble if moved from side to side, without appearing liquid. Remove the ramekins from the roasting dish and leave them to cool to room temperature.

Gently heat the sugar for the caramel in a small saucepan until about half of it has liquified and started to colour, then gently stir it. Watch carefully, stirring frequently until it is a deep gold, then remove from the heat. Liberally dust the creams with icing sugar using a tea strainer, then drizzle a teaspoon of caramel over each one. It should set hard within minutes. Cover and chill for a couple of hours.

blueberry compote

An alternative to the caramel top is to serve crème brûlée with a fruit compote, blueberries for instance. Place 250g blueberries and 50g caster sugar in a small pan over a low heat, and gently cook for 5–8 minutes, stirring occasionally, until the sugar has melted and formed a syrup with the juice from the blueberries. Transfer the fruit and syrup to a bowl, add a squeeze of lemon juice, and leave to cool. Spoon the blueberries and syrup over the crème brûlées – you can do this before or after chilling.

A light healthy girl's pud, one that's also yummy mid-morning with an espresso. For the full crunch, it needs to be eaten soon after it's assembled, but you can always make up the yogurt in advance. It's still very good once the oats soften though, and in this case cover and chill it.

layered passionfruit and yogurt crunch

500g Greek yogurt
50g icing sugar, sifted
1 tablespoon lemon juice
2 passionfruit, halved
50g granola

Serves 4

Blend the yogurt with the icing sugar and lemon juice. Spoon half of this into the base of four 180ml glasses, spoon half the passionfruit seeds over, then scatter with the granola. Spoon the remaining yogurt on top and drizzle over the rest of the passionfruit seeds.

Don't take the name too literally, but this does stand the test of a few days in the fridge, firming up as time goes on. Its charm hasn't dimmed since its heyday – it's certainly been around since my childhood – and it's hard to see it ever going away.

What has disappeared however are those blocks of chocolate chip mint ice cream, a resoundingly fond memory, that I sometimes summon up by stirring tiny splinters of dark chocolate into the syllabub, which has the same appeal.

Using a large sharp knife, finely slice 40g dark chocolate into splinters. Set aside a scant tablespoon, and fold in the remainder, then scatter a little of the reserved chocolate into the centre of each one before chilling.

everlasting lemon syllabub

Juice of 1 lemon

1 heaped teaspoon finely grated
   lemon zest

2 tablespoons brandy

50g caster sugar

200ml double cream

100ml sweet white wine

Jellied lemon slices to decorate

Cigarettes russes or other delicate
   biscuits to serve (optional)

Serves 4

Place the lemon juice, the zest, brandy and the sugar in a bowl and leave for at least 2 hours. Stir the mixture to dissolve the sugar, but don't worry if it doesn't dissolve completely.

Whip the cream in a bowl until it just starts to hold its shape; I use a hand-held electric whisk, and add the wine in about three goes, whisking between each addition. If the wine is added too quickly the mixture can split, so it's important to do it gradually. Finally add the lemon and sugar mixture and whisk to a thick, fluffy syllabub.

Spoon into glasses, decorate with a couple of lemon slices, cover and chill for several hours. The syllabub will keep well in the fridge for several days. Serve with cigarettes russes, or some other lacy biscuit if wished.

This almost has the edge over a crème brûlée (see page 86) – it's not as rich, but the caramel is a sure fire thing, the easiest part of it. Don't stint on the vanilla here, the sacrifice of a whole pod is eminently worth it, a light wobbly custard laced with tiny seeds.

crème caramel

Custard

700ml milk
1 vanilla pod, slit
5 large eggs
75g caster sugar

Caramel

120g caster sugar (refined)
2 tablespoons water

Serves 6

Pour the milk into a small pan. Open out the vanilla pod and scrape out the seeds with a small sharp knife; add these to the milk with the pod. Bring to the boil, then remove from the heat and leave to infuse while you make the caramel.

Place the sugar for the caramel in another small pan with the water. Bring to the boil, and stir now and again until the sugar has dissolved, then simmer until it turns a deep toffee-apple gold, stirring as it begins to colour at the edges. Pour it over the base of six small bowls or 150ml ramekins and leave to harden for about 15 minutes.

Preheat the oven to 130°C fan/150°C/gas mark 2. Bring the milk back to the boil. Whisk the eggs and sugar for the custard in a large bowl, then whisk on the hot milk, and pass it through a sieve into another bowl. Place the ramekins in a roasting dish, pour the custard on top of the caramel using a jug. Pour cold water into the roasting dish that comes two-thirds of the way up the sides of the ramekins, and bake for 1 hour. Remove the ramekins from the roasting dish, run a small sharp knife around the top of each ramekin, and carefully peel off the skin. Loosely cover with clingfilm and leave to cool, then cover and chill for several hours. They keep well for a couple of days.

To serve, run a knife around the edge of each crème caramel, place a plate on top and invert.

trifles

Trifles are a deep-sea dive, down through a glassy surface of cream and custard to an underworld of hidden treasures that ends in a booze-soaked syrupy bed of sponge. Over the centuries they have been shaped by fashion, and bizarrely come full circle. If the intervening years at the turn of the twentieth century saw 'de trop' trifles that called for three different types of jam, as well as marmalade and several types of wine and liqueur, today the finest reflect the eighteenth-century tradition of Hannah Glasse's day of custard topped with a layer of syllabub.

I have always loved making – or rather creating – trifles. Their forte lies with the artistic licence of dreaming up the different layers. The bottom layer can be anything that's willing to soak up the liquor. Trifle sponges are obviously designed for the task, sweet and so dry you would never dream of eating them on their own. And sponge fingers are another material, or it could be a light sponge cake for something truly soft. I particularly like the contemporary touch of using jam Swiss roll slices, propped upright like wheels around the edge of the bowl, that wittily takes care of two ingredients in one.

Then there's the booze, the jam, the fruit, the amaretti for that vintage savour once provided by Ratafia biscuits, and the deep deep bank of whatever syllabub, custard or whipped cream you have chosen. An all-singing, all-dancing trifle will have at least two if not three of these creamy layers, but that's going to take you several hours to assemble. And if it has to be just one, then my vote goes to syllabub, featherlight and laced with sweet wine and liqueurs, with the advantage of slowly giving these sublime liquids up to the sponge in the day or two after it's made. So while the sponge softens the syllabub firms to a mousse, making it a triumph to eat after a spell slumbering in the fridge.

There is something of the age of innocence about this trifle. Its simplicity takes me back to the trifles my mother used to make. If there is any difference it is the syllabub in lieu of custard – light and fluffy, and heady with sweet sherry and liqueur.

old-fashioned sherry trifle

Trifle

4 oranges (medium rather
   than navel)
30g caster sugar
6 trifle sponges
120g seedless raspberry jam

Syllabub

Finely grated zest of 1 orange,
   plus 2 tablespoons juice
Good squeeze of lemon juice
120ml sweet sherry
2 tablespoons Cointreau
50g icing sugar
300ml double cream

To decorate

Soft amaretti
Icing sugar for dusting
Gold or silver dragees (optional)

Serves 8

To make the trifle, halve and juice 2 of the oranges, and reduce with the sugar in a small pan over a medium heat to give 50ml of syrup. Arrange the trifle sponges on the base of a 20cm trifle dish at least 8cm deep, cutting to fit and squeezing them in. Splash the syrup over. Place the jam in a bowl and work it with a spoon until smooth, then spread it over the sponges.

Slice off the skin and outer pith from the remaining 2 oranges and run a small sharp knife between the segments to remove them from the membranes. Drain the segments into a sieve over a bowl, then scatter them over the trifle sponges.

To make the syllabub, whisk the orange zest and juice with the lemon juice, sherry, Cointreau and icing sugar in a large bowl. Slowly whisk in the cream and continue to whisk until you have a light and fluffy syllabub. While it needs to be the consistency of softly whipped cream, take care not to overwhisk otherwise it can separate; I use a hand-held electric whisk. Smooth the syllabub over the trifle base. Cover with clingfilm and chill overnight. During this time the syllabub will firm up, and the juices will soak into the sponge. Just before serving, decorate with amaretti, a dusting of icing sugar and dragees if you wish.

easy trifle

Arrange 4–6 trifle sponges over the base of a trifle dish and drizzle over 4–6 tablespoons of medium-dry sherry. Stir 300g sliced strawberries into 150g strawberry jam and spoon two-thirds over the sponges. Whisk a 500g tub of custard with 225g clotted cream and smooth on top. Chill until required, spooning the remaining strawberries over just before serving. Serves 6.

Jam Swiss rolls could have been custom-made to line the base of a trifle, a ready-made all-in-one of sponge and jam that couldn't look prettier standing up like wheels round the inside of a glass bowl. I prefer to leave the stones in the cherries in this recipe to preserve the maiden whiteness of the cream, and the plump fruit give the trifle a wholesome rusticity.

strawberry and cherry trifle with almonds

Trifle
400g jam Swiss roll
2 tablespoons amaretto
150g strawberry jam
300g strawberries, hulled

Syllabub
Finely grated zest of 1 orange,
    plus 2 tablespoons juice
Good squeeze of lemon juice
120ml sweet wine
2 tablespoons brandy
50g icing sugar
300ml double cream

To decorate
200g cherries
25g toasted flaked almonds*
icing sugar for dusting

Serves 6

Line the sides of a 20cm trifle dish at least 8cm deep with 2cm-thick slices of Swiss roll, placed upright, then cut the remainder 3–4cm thick and line the base. Splash the amaretto over. Press the jam through a sieve into a bowl, slice the strawberries then fold them into the jam. Spoon this over the central sponges.

To make the syllabub, whisk the orange zest and juice with the lemon juice, sweet wine, brandy and icing sugar in a large bowl. Slowly whisk in the cream in a thin stream, and continue to whisk until you have a light and fluffy syllabub. While it needs to be the consistency of softly whipped cream, take care not to overwhisk otherwise it can separate; I use a hand-held electric whisk. Smooth the syllabub over the trifle base. Cover with clingfilm and chill overnight. During this time the syllabub will firm up, and the juices will soak into the sponge.

Just before serving, decorate with the cherries and almonds and a dusting of icing sugar.

*To toast almonds, scatter them over the base of a small baking dish and toast for 8–10 minutes in an oven preheated to 180°C fan/200°C/gas mark 6.

traditional trifle

Replace the Swiss roll with 6 trifle sponges, cutting to fit and squeezing them in.

Deliciously silky and cooling, one for those who reckon the best bits of a trifle are the boozy cake and custard and can pass on the jam and fruit. Though you could also scatter a handful of raspberries or blackberries over each bowl. Do buy your cake if you don't have anything homemade to hand, though try to avoid those mass-produced sponges: you want something with a little integrity.

italian trifle

6 large egg yolks

125g icing sugar, sifted

75g plain flour, sifted

650ml full-cream milk

3 strips of lemon peel

1½ teaspoons vanilla extract

4 tablespoons dark rum

250g plain sponge or Madeira cake,
    cut into 1cm slices

Cocoa powder for dusting

Serves 6

Whisk the egg yolks and icing sugar together in a medium non-stick pan until smooth, and then whisk in the flour a third at a time, until you have a thick creamy paste.

Bring the milk to the boil in a small pan with the lemon peel, and whisk it into the egg mixture a little at a time initially, until it is all incorporated. Return the pan to a low heat and cook for a few minutes until the custard thickens, stirring vigorously with a wooden spoon to disperse any lumps that form, if necessary you can give it a quick whisk. The custard shouldn't actually boil, but the odd bubble will ensure it's hot enough to thicken properly. Cook it for a few minutes longer, again stirring constantly. Remove the custard from the heat and stir in the vanilla and half the rum. Discard the lemon zest, pour the custard into a bowl, cover the surface with clingfilm and leave to cool.

To assemble the trifle, give the custard a stir with a spoon to smooth it, then spread a couple of tablespoons over the base of a 20cm trifle dish 8cm deep (it can also be assembled in individual glass dishes). Break up some of the sliced cake and arrange on the base of the bowl to partially cover it. Sprinkle over a little of the remaining rum, then smooth over a third of the custard. Repeat until you have three layers of cake and three of custard, ending with custard. Cover the trifle with clingfilm and chill for at least 2 hours. It can also be made the night before.

To serve, liberally dust the surface with cocoa using a tea strainer.

Every now and again I chance upon quinces outside the Middle Eastern shops close by where I live, but for the most part rely on membrillo or quince paste when I need something of this perfumed fruit. You can use brandy if you don't have Poire William.

pear and quince trifle

300ml water

180g caster sugar

1 vanilla pod, slit, or 1 teaspoon
   vanilla extract

2 Comice pears

2 tablespoons Poire William

70g sponge fingers

100g membrillo

1 tablespoon lemon juice

Syllabub

Finely grated zest of 1 orange,
   plus 2 tablespoons juice

Good squeeze of lemon juice

125ml sweet wine

2 tablespoons Cointreau

50g icing sugar

300ml double cream

To decorate

15g toasted flaked almonds
   (see page 97)

Serves 6–8

Place the water, the sugar and vanilla in a small pan and bring to the boil. Peel and halve the pears, add them to the syrup so that as far as possible they are submerged. Cover with a circle of baking paper and poach until the pears are tender when pierced with a skewer, this can take 4–15 minutes depending on their ripeness. Allow them to cool in the syrup, then remove and drain thoroughly, quarter, core and finely slice them lengthwise. Mix 2 tablespoons of the syrup with the Poire William eau-de-vie.

Arrange the sponge fingers sugared-side up on the base of a 20cm trifle dish at least 7cm deep, drizzle over the brandied syrup, and scatter the pears on top. Gently heat the membrillo with the lemon juice in a small pan, working it with a spoon until it's smooth and melted. Smear this over the pears.

To make the syllabub, whisk the orange zest and juice with the squeeze of lemon juice, sweet wine, Cointreau and icing sugar in a bowl. Slowly whisk in the cream, and continue to whisk until you have a light and fluffy syllabub. While it needs to be the consistency of whipped cream, take care not to overwhisk otherwise it can separate; I use a hand-held electric whisk. Pour the syllabub over the trifle and smooth the surface, cover with clingfilm and chill for several hours or ideally overnight. (You can in fact make it up to two days beforehand.) During this time the syllabub will firm up, and the juices will soak into the sponge.

To serve, scatter the almonds over the surface.

A trifle full of wintery sentiments, that looks to Scotland for inspiration from its famed pud of toasted oatmeal and whisky.

cranachan trifle

3 trifle sponges, sliced
100g raspberry jam
250g raspberries
150g flapjacks, crumbled
   (see below)

Syllabub
finely grated zest of 1 orange,
   plus 100ml smooth fresh
   orange juice
50ml whisky
50g icing sugar, plus extra for
   dusting (optional)
300ml double cream

Serves 6–8

Arrange the sliced sponges over the base of a 20cm trifle dish at least 8cm deep. Work the jam until smooth, then stir in the raspberries, reserving a few for decoration. Spoon this over the sponge, then scatter over the flapjacks.

To make the syllabub, whisk the orange zest and juice with the whisky and icing sugar in a large bowl. Slowly whisk in the cream in a thin stream, and continue to whisk until you have a light and fluffy syllabub. While it needs to be the consistency of softly whipped cream, take care not to overwhisk otherwise it can separate; I use a hand-held electric whisk. Smooth the syllabub over the trifle base. Cover with clingfilm and chill overnight. During this time the syllabub will firm up, and the juices will soak into the sponge.

Just before serving, decorate with a few raspberries, and a dusting of icing sugar if wished.

flapjacks

For divinely chewy flapjacks, preheat the oven to 160°C fan/180°C/gas mark 4. Gently melt 240g diced salted butter with 180g demerara sugar and 6 tablespoons golden syrup in a medium pan over a medium heat. Stir in 350g rolled oats (I prefer processed ones here to anything too butch and nutty). Tip the mixture into a 23cm square tin or equivalent size, pressing it down, and bake for 20 minutes. Leave to cool and then cut into squares.

This is summer pudding in trifle form, which I think I could come to love even more than the classic. It's that much easier to make, and less at risk of those niggling little patches of undyed white bread that can occasionally mar a summer pudding. Sponge fingers are layered with the compote and soak up all the juices, and the whole thing is smothered in cream.

summer pudding trifle

500g redcurrants
170g caster sugar
700g raspberries,
    plus a few extra to decorate
About 130g sponge fingers
300ml double cream,
    whipped to soft peaks
Icing sugar for dusting (optional)

Serves 6

String the currants into a small pan using a fork, add the sugar and gently heat together, stirring occasionally, for 4–6 minutes until the fruit is soft but still retains its shape, and is sitting in a pool of syrup. Place half the currants in a sieve and press the juice into a bowl and then return it to the pan, discarding the solids. Fold in the raspberries, stir well and heat very gently for a minute or two, not to cook them but to encourage them to release their juices, gently turning them once. Transfer the compote to a bowl and leave to cool.

Arrange half the sponge fingers over the base of a 20cm trifle dish 8–9cm deep. Spoon half of the compote over the sponge, then repeat with the remaining sponge fingers and compote. Cover and chill for a couple of hours, then smooth the cream over the surface, cover and chill for another couple of hours or overnight.

Just before serving, decorate with a few raspberries, and if you like, give them a flurry of icing sugar.

all-white trifle

Sponge

4 medium organic egg whites
Pinch of sea salt
½ teaspoon cream of tartar
125g icing sugar, sifted
70g plain flour, sifted

Trifle

1 x 400g tin pears in syrup
3 tablespoons Poire William
    or brandy
6 meringue nests (80g), crumbled

Mousse

500g mascarpone
4 medium organic egg whites
50g caster sugar
1 vanilla pod, slit,
    or 1 teaspoon vanilla extract

To decorate

6 amaretti
1 tablespoon toasted flaked or
    slivered almonds (see page 97)
Icing sugar for dusting

Sauce

200g blackcurrant jam
1 tablespoon lemon juice

Serves 6–8

Preheat the oven to 150°C fan/170°C/gas mark 3. Whisk the egg whites in a large bowl with the salt and cream of tartar until risen; I use a hand-held electric whisk. Sprinkle in the sugar a couple of tablespoons at a time, whisking for about 20 seconds with each addition. Fold the sifted flour into the meringue in two goes, then transfer the mixture to a buttered 20cm cake tin at least 5cm deep with a removeable base. Bake the sponge for 30–35 minutes until lightly golden on the surface, springy to the touch, and shrinking from the sides. Run a knife around the edge of the cake and leave it to cool. Slice off its top with a bread knife, then cut it off the base of the tin and trim the sides so you are left with all white sponge. Cut this into two thin layers with the bread knife.

Mix 5 tablespoons of the pear syrup with the Poire William eau-de-vie or brandy, and sprinkle half of it over the meringues in a bowl. Thinly slice the pears. To prepare the mousse, beat the mascarpone in a bowl until smooth and creamy. If it seems hard, whizz it in the bowl of a food processor. In another bowl, whisk the egg whites until they hold their shape, then gradually sprinkle over the sugar and whisk well with each addition until you have a glossy meringue. Fold this in three goes into the mascarpone until you have a fluffy mousse. Open out the vanilla pod, scrape out the seeds with a small sharp knife, and work them into the mousse, or stir in the extract.

To assemble, smear a spoon of the mousse over the base of a 20cm glass bowl 8cm deep. Lay one cake layer on top and sprinkle over half the remaining brandied syrup. Scatter over half the meringue, half the pears, and smooth over a scant half of the mousse to allow plenty for the top. Repeat with the remaining ingredients. Cover and chill for at least 2 hours (or it can be made a day or two in advance).

Shortly before serving, pile the amaretti in the centre, scatter over the flaked almonds, then dust with icing sugar. To make the sauce, spoon the jam into a bowl and give it a stir, then blend in the lemon juice. Serve with the trifle.

In this variation on a traditional theme, a mascarpone mousse stands in for custard or syllabub, bringing it right up to the present day on our chronological calendar of the evolution of these lovely puds, by borrowing from the Italian pantry.

modern sherry trifle

6 trifle sponges
100ml sweet sherry
200g blackcurrant jam
1 tablespoon lemon juice
2 large oranges

Mousse
3 medium organic eggs, separated
50g caster sugar
400g mascarpone
½ teaspoon vanilla extract
  (optional)

To decorate
Silver dragees, or toasted
  flaked almonds (see page 97),
  optional
Icing sugar (optional)
Silver balls (optional)

Serves 6–8

Arrange the trifle sponges over the base of a 20cm glass bowl at least 8cm deep, and sprinkle with the sherry. Combine the jam and lemon juice in a bowl and smooth it over the sponges. Cut the skin and outer pith off the oranges and run a sharp knife between the segments to remove them from the membranes. Scatter the segments over the jam.

To make the mousse, whisk the egg yolks and sugar in a bowl, then beat in the mascarpone, and vanilla extract if using. Whisk the egg whites until stiff; I use a hand-held electric whisk, and fold into the mascarpone base. Smooth this over the top of the trifle, cover and chill for several hours. It will keep well for a couple of days.

Shortly before serving, either scatter with silver dragees or toasted flaked almonds (dusting them with icing sugar) or with a few silver balls.

chocolate puds

Chocolate is the lowest common denominator that spans every age group, culture and occasion. It even draws in the 'no thank yous' who don't normally eat pudding. Starting with the smallest and travelling up, chocolate mousse, which consists simply of eggs and chocolate, is a pudding no one should feel any more ashamed of dishing up than strawberries and cream. A touch more sophisticated are the petit pots au chocolat – by definition edible silk that melts in the mouth. Either of these delectable little numbers can be spiced up with vanilla, cinnamon, eaux-de-vie and sticky liqueurs.

Before we get to hearty baked puds, there is a halfway house: chocolate fondant puddings are as delicious as they are clever. With a thin crust of fluffy sponge encasing a thick chocolate sauce they remind me of Lemon Surprise Pudding, which I have always suspected rose from the ashes of a failed soufflé. I can't help but feel that when someone first came up with 'Chocolate Fondant Pudding' they had simply underestimated the cooking time of a baked sponge – in which case, long may people continue to make mistakes in the kitchen.

A little more on the gutsy side is a tray-baked chocolate sponge that can be cut into hulking squares and served with lashings of salty caramel sauce. Finally, when you fancy a small chocolatey farewell to dinner with a cup of coffee, then a tiny sliver of chocolate torte – that nemesis moment – or a gooey brownie is the answer. You can always wrap up the leftover to send home for any offspring not included, which might even encourage them to allow your guests out again.

Petit pots have always had the sophisticated edge over chocolate mousse with their exquisitely silky texture, achieved here by combining dark chocolate with a little milk. These particular little pots have Spanish overtones with their hint of spice and a chocolate almond on top. But for diehard chocoholics you could serve them austerely, less the spice and decoration, and for that matter less the crème fraîche.

petit pots au chocolat

225ml double cream

180ml full-cream milk

4 medium organic egg yolks, whisked

90g milk chocolate, broken into pieces

150g dark chocolate (about 50% cocoa), broken into pieces

½ teaspoon vanilla extract

⅓ teaspoon ground cinnamon

120g crème fraîche

6 chocolate almonds (optional)

Serves 6

Bring the cream and milk to the boil in a small non-stick pan, and whisk it onto the egg yolks which should thicken into a thin custard instantly. Pass this through a sieve into a bowl, cover the surface with clingfilm and leave to cool.

Gently melt the chocolate in a large bowl set over a pan with a little simmering water in it. Whisk in the cooled custard in two goes, then stir in the vanilla and cinnamon. Divide this between six 150ml ramekins or other little pots or coffee cups of a similar size. Cover and chill for several hours. Drop a heaped teaspoon of crème fraîche on the top of each little pot and decorate with a chocolate almond if wished. Cover and chill for a further few hours or overnight.

However simple, you can't go wrong with chocolate mousse for pudding, whatever the occasion. Everybody loves it. It has an elementary appeal, there's no point in complicating it: chocolate, eggs and a little liquid something. The coffee suggested could just as well be brandy, Cointreau or Tia Maria. Of course it doesn't have to be dressed up, but here are some suggestions for serving it up at a party.

chocolate mousse

250g dark chocolate (about 50% cocoa), broken into pieces
6 medium organic eggs, separated
2 tablespoons strong black coffee
Chocolate coffee beans, thins or buttons to decorate (optional)
Cocoa for dusting
Cigarettes russes or other dessert biscuits to serve (optional)

Serves 6

Gently melt the chocolate in a large bowl set over a pan with a little simmering water in it. The melted chocolate should be at room temperature, so if necessary leave it to cool for a few minutes before stirring in the egg yolks and then the coffee.

In another large bowl, whisk the egg whites until they are stiff; I use a hand-held electric whisk. Mix a couple of tablespoons into the chocolate mixture to loosen it, then fold in the remainder in two goes, as lightly as possible.

Transfer the mousse to a serving bowl or individual bowls or glasses, smoothing the surface. Decorate with chocolate coffee beans, thins or buttons or simply dust with cocoa. Cover with clingfilm and chill for several hours or overnight until firm.

Serve with cigarettes russes or other little dessert biscuits if liked.

I first ate these at La Bastide de Moustiers, Alain Ducasse's enchanting small hotel in the hills of Provence. My husband and I were enjoying a lazy lunch one blue-skied September day, with crudités from the garden for dipping into pastes made from crushed local goat's cheeses and olives, and a pan of crayfish from the nearby mountain ravine, so fresh they could have swum over, when a whirlwind whipped up from nowhere and a helicopter landed within a few feet of our table, having whisked up the neighbouring table of diners from the baking plains below. So these little custards that we ate for pudding have always held 'another world' glamour for me. I seem to recall there was a little coffee custard in the equation too, and some shortbread biscuits scented with lavender. But we'll settle for the chocolate and vanilla versions served with Cadbury's choccie fingers.

black and white custards

500ml full-cream milk

500ml double cream

10 medium organic egg yolks

225g caster sugar

1 vanilla pod, cut up

90g dark chocolate (about 50% cocoa), chopped into small pieces

6 tablespoons each dark and white chocolate shavings

Icing sugar and cocoa powder for dusting

Chocolate fingers or mini florentines to serve (optional)

Serves 6

Preheat the oven to 140°C fan/160°C/gas mark 3. Bring the milk and the cream to the boil in a small non-stick pan. Whisk the egg yolks and the sugar together in a large bowl, and whisk in the boiled milk. Pour half into another bowl.

Add the vanilla pod to one and leave to infuse for 10 minutes. Add the chocolate to the other, and leave for a few minutes. Whisk and strain the different mixtures into heatproof bowls (I used four 400ml cupped bowls, to give me two of each flavour for sharing between six of us). Place them in a roasting dish with hot but not boiling water that comes two-thirds of the way up the sides, and bake for 1 hour 15 minutes. They should be set but may gently wobble if moved from side to side, without appearing liquid. Leave the custards to cool completely, then cover and chill for several hours or overnight.

Shortly before serving, scatter the dark chocolate shavings over the vanilla custard, and dust with icing sugar, and scatter the white chocolate shavings over the dark chocolate custard and dust with cocoa powder. Serve them with chocolate fingers or florentines for a treat.

While so many puds demand the respect of being left exactly as they are, tira-mi-su is just the opposite, a great formula with endless possibility to play around, like trifles. I realise that I'm risking the wrath of Italian gourmets here, and perhaps I should have called it something else. But tira-mi-su is basically a trifle. Here you have lady fingers soaked in boozy coffee, layered with chocolate mousse in lieu of the usual mascarpone one.

very chocolatey tira-mi-su

150ml strong black coffee, cooled

70ml kahlua or dark rum

1 x quantity chocolate mousse (see page 114)

About ½ x 200g packet sponge fingers

Cocoa for dusting

Serves 6

Combine the coffee and liqueur in a shallow bowl. Smear a couple of tablespoons of the chocolate mousse on the base of a 20cm bowl at least 6cm deep. Dip the sponge fingers into the coffee-liqueur mixture until the sponge just starts to yield between your fingers, but not so that it is totally sodden.

Cover the base of the bowl with a single layer of sponge fingers, smooth half of the mousse on top, then repeat with the remaining half of the ingredients. Cover the surface and chill for several hours or overnight. Dust with cocoa shortly before serving.

Halfway between a 'mousse' and 'petit pots', just in case you felt a need to bridge the gap. At Eastertime you can turn these into little surprise soufflés by dropping a mini cream egg into each ramekin before filling them. As my nine-year old put it "Nice touch, mum".

chilled chocolate soufflés

Gently melt the dark chocolate in a large bowl set over a pan with a little simmering water in it. Leave this to cool for a few minutes, then beat in the egg yolks and then gradually whisk in the cream, and the sugar. Whisk the egg whites until they are stiff in a large bowl using an electric whisk, and fold into the chocolate base in two or three goes.

Carefully pour the chocolate mixture into six 150ml ramekins. You may find it easiest to transfer the mixture to a jug first. Place the ramekins in a baking tray, loosely cover with clingfilm and chill for several hours or overnight until set. To serve, dust the edge of the soufflés with grated chocolate.

THE REAL THING If you want to go the whole hog of a soufflé that's risen above the surface of the dish, then cut out six strips of baking paper about 5cm by the width of the roll. Use these to make a collar for each ramekin, by attaching a piece of adhesive tape to one end and sticking it to the top of the ramekin, then tightly winding it around the bowl and sticking it in place. Fill the ramekins about 1cm above the rim to create the effect of a risen soufflé. In this case the mixture will make 4–5 little pots. Carefully peel off the paper collars before dusting with chocolate shavings.

175g dark chocolate (about 50% cocoa), broken into pieces
3 medium organic eggs, separated
350ml whipping cream
15g icing sugar, sifted
Grated dark chocolate to serve

Serves 6

If you are someone who judges all chocolate puds by 'nemesis moments' since first trying the River Café's seminal cake, then try this one for size. It might be second best, but it's not a bad imitation.

a nemesis moment

Cake

50g self-raising flour

50g light muscovado sugar

50ml groundnut oil

1 medium egg, separated

1 tablespoon espresso, or very strong
 black coffee, cooled

1 tablespoon milk

Filling

300g dark chocolate (about 50%
 cocoa), broken into pieces

4 medium eggs, separated

30g golden caster sugar

250g mascarpone

2 tablespoons kahlúa or very strong
 black coffee

Edible gold or silver decorations, e.g.
 buttons, dragees, chocolate stars,
 leaf, etc (optional)

Serves 6–8

Heat the oven to 170°C fan/190°C/gas mark 5 and butter a 20cm cake tin at least 4cm deep with a removeable base. Sift the flour and sugar into a medium bowl. Add the oil, the egg yolk, espresso and milk and beat with a wooden spoon until smooth. Whisk the egg white until stiff in another bowl (I use a hand-held electric whisk for this) and fold into the mixture in two goes. Spoon this into the prepared tin, covering the base evenly, and give the tin a couple of sharp taps on the worktop to allow any bubbles to rise. Bake for 12–15 minutes until lightly golden, firm when pressed and shrinking from the sides. Leave to cool.

Place the chocolate in a bowl set over a pan with a little simmering water in it and gently melt. Remove the bowl from the heat and leave the chocolate to cool to room temperature if necessary. Whisk the egg whites until stiff in a largish bowl using a hand-held electric whisk, then whisk the egg yolks and sugar in another bowl until very pale and mousse-like.

Add the mascarpone to the melted chocolate and blend, then fold in the egg yolk mixture, and then the egg whites in two goes. Stir in the kahlúa or coffee. Smooth the chocolate cream over the cake base, scatter over gold or silver decorations if wished, cover and chill for several hours or overnight.

Run a knife around the collar and remove it, and serve the torte in slices.

Fondant puddings have come to define everything that is decadent and alluring about chocolate, the way they ooze warm molten goo from around the cakey sides is a bit like having everything chocolatey you ever dreamed of poured into one fantasy: part dense fudgey cake and part thick sticky sauce. Conveniently they can also be prepared well in advance of dinner and popped into the oven ten minutes or so before you want them – for which you will love them even more.

chocolate fondant puddings

300g dark chocolate (70% cocoa),
   broken into pieces
75g unsalted butter, diced
75g light muscovado sugar,
   plus extra for dusting
5 medium organic eggs
40g plain flour, sifted
1 tablespoon dark rum (optional)
Vanilla ice cream or crème fraîche
   to serve

Serves 6

Preheat the oven to 180°C fan/200°C electric/gas mark 6 and butter six 150ml ramekins. Gently melt the chocolate in a large bowl set over a pan with a little simmering water in it.

Place the butter, sugar, eggs and flour in the bowl of a food processor and whizz to a smooth batter, then add the melted chocolate and whizz again. Finally add the rum, if including. Divide the mixture between the dishes, dust with a little more sugar using a tea strainer, place on a baking sheet and bake for 9 minutes, until just starting to rise. There should be a thin rim of cooked cake on the outside, and a sticky river of molten goo inside.

Serve straight away, with either ice cream or crème fraîche. The cake mixture can also be prepared several hours in advance, in which case cover and chill the little dishes, and bake for 11–12 minutes.

Even though salted caramel seems to be flavour of the month, it's been a tradition in Brittany for years. I've long bought salted caramels in Normandy, and my local deli also sells jars of unctuously soft salted caramel for spreading on toast, something like a dulce de leche. So here we have a great big steaming tray of chocolate sponge, crusty and sugary around the top, with the hit of a sauce laced with molasses-rich sugar and crystalline sea salt.

salty caramel chocolate sponge

225g unsalted butter, diced
225g golden granulated sugar,
    plus 2 tablespoons
3 medium eggs
150ml milk
175g self-raising flour, sifted
50g cocoa, sifted
1½ teaspoons baking powder,
    sifted

Sauce
100g dark muscovado sugar
100g salted butter
150ml double cream

Makes 30 x 23cm cake
Serves in excess of 8

Preheat the oven to 170°C fan/190°C electric/gas mark 5 and butter a 30 x 23 x 4cm baking tin. Place the butter and the 225g sugar in the bowl of a food processor and beat together until pale and fluffy. Incorporate the eggs one at a time, scraping down the sides of the bowl if necessary, then add the milk. Don't worry if the mixture appears curdled at this point. Gradually add the flour, cocoa and baking powder through the funnel with the motor running.

Transfer the mixture to the baking tin, smoothing the surface. Scatter over a couple of tablespoons of sugar and bake for 30 minutes until golden and shrinking slightly from the sides, and a skewer comes out clean from the centre. Allow to cool for 20–30 minutes out of the oven, while you make the sauce. Heat the sugar, butter and cream in a small pan, whisking them until smooth.

Serve the cake cut into squares with the warm caramel sauce spooned over.

I felt I had to include this recipe, partly because I feel these are the best brownies I've ever cooked, but also because a small sliver of brownie makes a great end to lunch or dinner when you want a sugary little something without going the whole hog of getting out the pudding bowls and spoons. Actually, it doesn't even have to be little: pile them high and wide on the biggest plate you can find.

When I say 'good', that is within the context of an addiction to Gü® brownies and that dense texture so fudgey it leaves teethmarks. The secret here is to bake them for just 20 minutes, until they appear slightly cracked and risen around the outside but still gooey in the centre. Leave them to cool for a few hours and then chill for another few hours or overnight, et voilà, no one will know the difference between these and Gü® except these have pistachios in them, and even then the nuts are optional.

If, however, you want something soft and crumbly to eat slightly warm with a scoop of vanilla ice cream, then leave them in the oven that little bit longer, say 25–30 minutes in all, before sticking a skewer into the centre. This should come out clean with just a few moist crumbs clinging, without actually coating it.

pistachio brownies

Brownies

300g dark chocolate (about 50%
  cocoa), broken up
180g unsalted butter, diced
180g light muscovado sugar
4 medium eggs, and 1 egg yolk
115g ground almonds
¼ teaspoon sea salt
115g plain flour
1 heaped teaspoon baking powder
3 tablespoons fresh orange juice
75g shelled pistachios

Cream (optional)

75g white chocolate, broken up
½ tablespoon shelled pistachios
75ml whipping cream

Makes 16 brownies

Preheat the oven to 170°C fan/190°C electric/gas mark 5. You need a 23cm square tin, 4cm deep, or the equivalent. Provided it is non-stick there is no need to butter and flour it.

To make the brownies, gently melt the chocolate with the butter in a large bowl set over a pan with a little simmering water in it. Remove from the heat, add the sugar and stir to combine. Add the eggs and yolk to the chocolate mixture, one by one, beating after each addition, until the mixture is very glossy and amalgamated. Gently fold in the ground almonds and salt, then sift over the flour and baking powder and fold in without overmixing. Stir in the orange juice and fold in the pistachios.

Pour the mixture into the tin, and bake for 20–30 minutes (see introduction). Run a knife around the edge of the tin, leave the cake to cool for several hours, then cut it into 16 squares, or half that size for children's portions.

The brownies will be delicious as they are, but if you want to take them one step further, gently melt the white chocolate in a large bowl set over a pan with a little simmering water in it, then remove and leave to cool to room temperature. Finely crush the pistachios, either using a pestle and mortar or in a food processor. Whisk the cream until it is stiff, then gently fold in the cooled melted chocolate. Spoon a rounded teaspoon of this on top of each brownie and crown with a little crushed pistachio. The brownies will keep well in an airtight container for several days, though it is best to scatter over the nuts close to the time of eating.

pies and crumbles

Time to put on Johnny Cash's 'Live At St Quentin' and take your place in the rocker. Pies and crumbles are rooted in the homestead, thick quilts, open fires, and cosying down. They're rough around the edges and that's the appeal: we wouldn't have them any other way. That said, I couldn't resist including a recipe for the Dorchester's apple crumble just to show what happens when they get dressed for a night on the town.

Pies are firmly headed in the earth-mother direction, the flour-dusty frilled pinny of the kitchen. Deep red plums vie for place with Bramley apples to make one of the most sumptuous pies, slightly soggy pastry on the base and lashings of rich vanilla custard. Not that pies have to mean pastry, a thick bank of sponge sprinkled with crunchy sugar is another walk down Easy Street. Two of my standbys are apple sponge baked in a thin buttery syrup that thickens into a caramel sauce as it cooks, and a rhubarb sponge, the fruit hidden beneath a crusty cake wafting steam as you cut into it.

In real terms, a crumble is like a pastry that hasn't made it into a ball; a deconstructed biscuit laced with butter and sugar, with all the ease that suggests. Its loose texture comes with the potential for adding a smattering of character by way of some oats, nuts, or a little spice.

Summer is almost better than winter for this genre of pud: juicy red berries, peaches, apricots and plums are all winners. Evenings are almost always chilly unless you're in the tropics, and a pie or crumble can round off a candle-lit dinner on the terrace in a more welcome way than something flimsy. Lastly, cooked fruit is at its most fragrant 20–30 minutes out of the oven, and still on fine form once cool, so you can cook these in advance and settle back to the rocker with a good book.

A big no-nonsense apple pie, 100 percent nurture, you can almost see the curl of steam rising from its centre as a slipper-clad Mamma carries it to the table. Custard it has to be here.

big apple pie

Sweet pastry

150g unsalted butter, softened
150g caster sugar
2 medium eggs
400g plain flour, sifted,
  plus 1 tablespoon
50g ground almonds

Apples

900g (3 good-sized) Bramley
  apples, peeled, cored
  and sliced
125g light brown sugar
½ teaspoon ground cinnamon
Finely grated zest of 1 lemon, plus
  juice of ½ lemon
25g unsalted butter
Caster sugar for dusting

Serves 4

To make the pastry, cream the butter and sugar together in a bowl using a wooden spoon until soft and fluffy. A food processor or mixer will make light work of this. Beat in the eggs until well combined, then gradually add the 400g flour and ground almonds and bring the dough together. Wrap it in clingfilm and chill for at least 2 hours; it will keep for several days.

Preheat the oven to 170°C fan/190°C/gas mark 5. Allow the dough to come to room temperature for a few minutes, and then knead until pliable. Thinly roll out two-thirds of the dough on a lightly floured surface. Use this to line the base of a shallow 30cm (2 litre) gratin dish or other shallow ovenproof dish, letting the extra hang over the sides, then trim off the excess. Don't worry if the dough tears and you end up partly pressing it into the dish. Sprinkle the tablespoon of flour over the apples in a bowl and toss, then mix in the brown sugar, spice, lemon zest and juice. Tip the apples into the dish, arranging them evenly, and dot with the butter. Roll out the remaining third of pastry with the trimmings, and lay it over the top. As the pastry is quite short and delicate, I find it easiest to wrap it around the rolling pin and lift it up. Press the pastry together at the rim and trim, leaving 1cm for shrinkage, then crimp the edge using the tip of your finger or the tip of a knife. Cut several diagonal slits in the surface and dust with caster sugar. Bake the pie for 40 minutes until golden.

This one's a British aristocrat; rhubarb makes for one of the finest crumbles of all – as do gooseberries during their brief season. It emerges from the oven, its sticky sweet and sour pink juices bubbling like a lazy geyser at the sides, with the promise of the meltingly tender fruit peppered with candied ginger concealed beneath.

rhubarb crumble

800g rhubarb (trimmed
   weight), cut into 3cm
   lengths
200g self-raising flour,
   plus 2 tablespoons

200g demerara sugar
2 knobs stem ginger, coarsely
   chopped
100g ground almonds
175g unsalted butter,
   chilled and diced

Serves 6

Preheat the oven to 180°C fan/200°C/gas mark 6.

Toss the rhubarb in a bowl with the 2 tablespoons of flour, half the sugar and the ginger and arrange over the base of a 30cm (2 litre) oval gratin or other shallow ovenproof dish.

Combine the flour, remaining sugar and ground almonds in a bowl and rub in the butter until you have large crumbs. This can also be done in a food processor, but take care to stop the motor before it turns the crumbs into a dough. Scatter this mixture over the fruit, and bake for 30–35 minutes until the top is golden and crisp, and juices are bubbling up at the sides.

Serve about 20–30 minutes out of the oven. It's also delicious cold.

peach and pistachio crisp

The most relaxed take on this genre, this one's half baked fruit and half crumble – peaches in a rose-scented syrup with just a smattering of biscuity nibs scattered over.

115g golden caster sugar

1 tablespoon rosewater

3 peaches

75g plain flour

75g unsalted butter, diced

50g shelled pistachios
  (unsalted)

Crème fraîche to serve (optional)

Serves 6

Preheat the oven to 180°C fan/200°C/gas mark 6.

Pour 100ml boiling water over 40g of the sugar in a bowl and stir to dissolve, then stir in the rosewater.

Halve the peaches and twist to separate them. Remove the stones; if they don't come out easily use a small sharp knife. Arrange the halves cut-side up in a shallow baking dish (I use a 30cm oval gratin dish) and pour the syrup over the peaches and into the base of the dish.

Place the remaining sugar, flour, butter and pistachios in the bowl of a food processor and reduce to a crumble. Keep the motor running until the mixture starts to cling together into lumps. Scatter over the crumble: don't worry if some falls to the bottom of the dish. Bake for 40 minutes until golden and crisp on top. There should be a delicious syrupy crumble surrounding the peach halves as well. Serve about 15 minutes out of the oven with a spoon of crème fraîche, if wished, or at room temperature.

I have always harboured a love of flapjacks, and here gooey chunks are served crumble-style on a succulent base of apricots and blueberries. It's even easier to make than a crumble; simply fold oats into melted butter and syrup and you're there.

apricot and blueberry flapjack

150g unsalted butter
150g golden syrup
$^1/_2$ teaspoon sea salt
180g rolled oats
8 ripe apricots
200g blueberries
2 tablespoons light muscovado sugar

Serves 6

Preheat the oven to 180°C fan/200°C/gas mark 6.

Gently melt the butter in a small pan with the syrup and the salt, then fold in the oats.

Quarter the apricots, removing the stones, and arrange with the blueberries in the base of a 30cm (2 litre) oval gratin or other shallow ovenproof dish. Sprinkle with the sugar, and then scatter over the flapjack mixture. There should still be some fruit showing through. Bake for 30 minutes until the top is golden and crusty. Serve about 10 minutes out of the oven. It's also delicious cold.

Pistachios and sour cherries are the wild cards here, in a crumble that goes from biscuit-crisp on the very top, steadily giving up the fight as you travel down to where it meets the fruit, where it soaks up the pear juices.

pear and sour cherry crumble

Fruit

900g pears, peeled, quartered, cored
   and thinly sliced
1 tablespoon lemon juice
50g demerara sugar
75g dried sour cherries

Crumble

200g plain flour
200g porridge oats
200g demerara sugar
200g unsalted butter, chilled
   and diced
75g shelled pistachios

Crème fraîche to serve

Serves 6–8

Preheat the oven to 170°C fan/190°C/gas mark 5. Toss the pears in a large bowl with the lemon juice and sugar, then gently mix in the sour cherries. Arrange the fruit in a shallow 30cm (2 litre) oval gratin or ovenproof dish.

Combine the flour, oats, sugar and butter in a food processor, and whizz until the mixture resembles large crumbs, taking care to stop the motor before it turns into a dough. Transfer the crumble to a bowl, then mix in the nuts. Scatter the mixture over the fruit, don't worry if you have to mound it, the crumble will sink as it cooks. Bake for 40 minutes until the top is golden and crisp. Serve the crumble 20–30 minutes out of the oven with a spoonful of crème fraîche. It's also delicious cold.

Plums are a fruit that I rarely eat raw, but would be my first choice to encounter beneath a lid of sweet buttery pastry. They relax into this richly flavoured compote when you cook them, spilling out sticky juices that soak into the pastry. And this is a particularly fine custard, that will lend itself to any of the crumbles and pies in this chapter. It doesn't have to be vanilla, a little cinnamon, ground cloves, cardamom or splash of liqueur can be used to bring out the best in whatever fruits are starring.

plum pie with vanilla custard

Sweet pastry

150g unsalted butter, softened
150g golden caster sugar
2 medium eggs
400g plain flour, sifted
50g ground almonds

Vanilla custard

300ml full-cream milk
6 medium organic egg yolks
75g golden caster sugar
1 vanilla pod, slit and cut up
150ml whipping cream

Plums

900g plums, stoned and quartered
125g light muscovado sugar
2 tablespoons plain flour
Finely grated zest of 1 lemon
Caster sugar for dusting

Serves 6

To make the pastry, cream the butter and sugar together in a bowl using a wooden spoon until soft and fluffy. A food processor will make light work of this. Beat in the eggs until well combined, then gradually add the flour and ground almonds and bring the dough together. Wrap it in clingfilm and chill for at least 2 hours; it will keep for several days.

To make the custard, pour the milk into a small pan and bring to the boil. Whisk the egg yolks and sugar in a bowl, then whisk in the milk. Return this to the pan and heat gently until you have a thin pouring custard that coats the back of the spoon, taking care not to overheat it. Pour it immediately into a bowl, add the vanilla pod, cover the surface with clingfilm and leave until cool. Liquidise the custard and pass it through a sieve, then whip the cream until it forms soft peaks and whisk it in. Cover and chill the custard until required, and give it a good stir before serving.

Toss the plums with 2 tablespoons of the sugar in a bowl and leave for 30 minutes to draw out any excess juice, then drain them. Preheat the oven to 180°C fan/ 200°C/gas mark 6. Allow the dough to come to room temperature for a few minutes, and then knead it until pliable. Thinly roll out two-thirds of the dough on a lightly floured surface. Use this to line the base of a 1.7 litre pie dish or oval gratin dish, letting the extra hang over the sides. Don't worry if the dough tears and you end up partly pressing it into the dish.

Toss the plums with the remaining sugar, the flour and lemon zest, and tip them into the pie dish. Roll out the remaining pastry with any trimmings, paint the pastry rim on the dish with milk and lay it on top. Press the pastry together, trim the sides, then crimp the edge using your fingertip or the tip of a knife. Brush the pastry with milk, cut several diagonal slits in the centre and dust with caster sugar. Bake for about 35 minutes until the pastry is golden and the plums are tender. Serve hot about 10 minutes out of the oven, or at room temperature, with the custard.

This is more cake than pie, a steaming scented sponge atop a fluffy mass of apples. And however unlikely it seems when you put it into the oven, don't be deterred: what appears to be an impossibly thin liquid at the start shapes up nicely into a luscious caramel that coats the sponge by the time the oven's done its stuff.

apple butterscotch pie

600g (2 good-sized) Bramley apples, peeled, quartered and sliced

Sponge

150g self-raising flour
50g caster sugar
80g unsalted butter, chilled and diced
1 medium egg
100ml milk
Finely grated zest of 1 lemon
50g currants

Sauce

80g light muscovado sugar
25g unsalted butter
100ml water
¼ teaspoon sea salt
juice of ½ lemon

Serves 6

Preheat the oven to 180°C fan/200°C/gas mark 6. To make the sponge, place the flour and sugar in a bowl, and rub in the butter; this can also be done in a food processor or mixer. Now incorporate the egg and the milk, then fold in the lemon zest and the currants. Arrange the apple in the base of a 30cm (2 litre) oval gratin or other shallow ovenproof dish and smooth the sponge mixture on top.

To make the sauce, place the sugar, butter, water and salt in a small pan and bring to the boil. Stir in the lemon juice, then pour this mixture over the pudding. The sauce will seem very liquid at this point, but once baked it transforms into a rich butterscotch. Bake the pudding for 30–35 minutes until golden on the surface and bubbling around the edges. Serve 5–10 minutes out of the oven.

Wherever school food failed, it made up for it with those big trays of cake sprinkled with sugar concealing just a little fruit in the name of goodness underneath. I prefer this kind of pud to a steamed sponge, not least because it has a lovely crusty golden surface, and, can be eaten cold as well as hot. In true comfort pudding style it's delicious with custard or crème fraîche.

baked rhubarb sponge

Fruit
600g forced rhubarb, trimmed
   and cut into 2cm lengths
125g golden caster sugar

Sponge
225g golden caster sugar
225g unsalted butter, diced
225g self-raising flour
2 teaspoons baking powder
4 medium eggs
100ml milk
Finely grated zest of 1 lemon

Serves 6–8

Preheat the oven to 180°C fan/200°C/gas mark 6. Toss the rhubarb with the sugar in a bowl and arrange over the base of a 30cm (2 litre) oval gratin dish or individual ovenproof dishes if you have them.

Reserving 2 tablespoons of the sugar, place all the sponge ingredients in the bowl of a food processor and cream together. Smooth this on top of the rhubarb, scatter over the reserved sugar and bake for 40 minutes. It's at its fluffiest and most scented served hot, but also good at room temperature.

Had you ever idly pondered on what a posh crumble is like, then this should satiate your curiosity. The crumble is that much finer, and the fruit cooks in a delectable butterscotch sauce. At the Dorchester this comes with all the trimmings: ripe autumn berries, whisky ice cream and a raspberry purée, which you're not expected to run to any more than you are to dress up to eat it.

the Dorchester's apple and sultana crumble

Fruit

150g caster sugar (refined)

60g unsalted butter

3 cooking apples (about 900g), peeled, cored and cut into 1cm dice

25g sultanas

25g raisins

½ teaspoon cinnamon

Crumble

75g light brown sugar

75g plain flour

75g ground almonds

75g unsalted butter

To serve (optional)

Whisky ice cream

120g autumn fruit (raspberries, blueberries, blackberries)

Raspberry purée

Serves 6

Preheat the oven to 170°C fan/190°C/gas mark 5. To prepare the caramel base for the fruit, place the caster sugar with 100ml water in a medium pan and simmer over a medium heat for 10– 15 minutes until a lovely toffee gold. Give it an initial stir to help the sugar dissolve, and again as it begins to colour. Now add the butter in small pieces, stirring well with each addition until incorporated; by the end you should have a thick butterscotch sauce. Add the apples and cook for 4–5 minutes. Initially the sauce will sieze up, but as you continue to heat the pan it will melt again. Stir in the sultanas, raisins and cinnamon and transfer to a 30cm (2 litre) oval gratin dish or other shallow ovenproof dish.

Place all the ingredients for the crumble in the bowl of a food processor and whizz until the mixture resembles fine crumbs. Evenly scatter this over the fruit and bake for 40 minutes until lightly golden and the fruit is bubbling through at the edges.

Serve with all the trimmings if you wish, though the crumble is delicious just as it is.

good old-fashioned

I think it's highly unlikely that we will ever forget the traditional puds we grew up with, regardless of trends and fashions. We might tweak them, pare them down or glam them up, even give the occasional new one the honour of becoming a tradition, but they are writ large in our memories and most of us cling tenaciously to the nostalgia they recall.

Bread and butter pudding is one of the Holy Grails of the kitchen; chefs and cooks throughout the land pride themselves on making the best one around. It has now surpassed its humble beginnings as a parsimonious guise for using up yesterday's bread, enriched with a little butter and soaked in milk, eggs and sugar, to emerge in gloriously rich versions with a lightly set creamy custard surrounding panettone, brioche or a country bread spread with marmalade, a whole vanilla pod in its midst. And not any old dried fruit: it has to be soaked in brandy or rum.

One needs a good rice pudding up one's sleeve too. Ideally an ambrosial cool creamy rice that can secretly be dipped into during the early hours of the morning, and at other times of the day can be scattered with all manner of fruits, from pomegranate seeds to passion fruit.

But perhaps the new national favourite is Sticky Toffee Pudding, a steaming sponge rich with dates, and an unctuous toffee sauce. As you might expect from a pudding of this popularity there are several contenders to the throne of invention. But Francis Coulson of the Sharrow Bay Country House Hotel in Penrith, just south of the Scottish border, who called it 'icky sticky toffee sponge' is the man who launched it on the nation, back in 1960. How nice to think that all those hippies had great puds as well as rock 'n' roll and free love to get them through that punishing decade.

Its name precedes it and says it in one. It was, after all, once called 'icky sticky toffee pudding' after that lovely molasses rich sauce that smothers the date sponge.

sticky toffee pudding

Sponge
150g pitted dates, chopped
250ml water
2 teaspoons bicarbonate of soda
75g unsalted butter, diced
125g light muscovado sugar
2 medium eggs
2 tablespoons golden syrup
1 teaspoon vanilla extract
200g plain flour, sifted

Sauce
100g dark muscovado sugar
100g unsalted butter
150ml double cream
Double cream or crème fraîche to serve

Serves 6–8

Preheat the oven to 170°C fan/190°C/gas mark 5 and butter a 27 x 18cm traybake or cake tin.

Bring the dates and water to the boil in a small pan and simmer over a low heat for 5 minutes. Remove from the heat and stir in the bicarbonate of soda, which will froth up.

Cream the butter and sugar together in a food processor, add the eggs one at a time, and then the syrup, vanilla, and flour. Transfer the mixture to a large bowl and beat in the date mixture in two goes. Pour the mixture into the prepared tin and bake for 25 minutes until the top is set and the cake is risen and shrinking from the sides.

Meanwhile make the sauce. Heat the sugar, butter and cream together in a small pan, whisking until smooth. Smooth half the sauce over the top of the cake and cut it into squares. Offer the remaining sauce separately for those that like lots. Serve with plenty of cream.

This talks to the Brit in us, regardless of whether you derive from these isles, it's for everyone who loves toast and marmalade. The custard here is made with egg yolks, fresh orange juice, cream and sugar, and is richly flavoured and lightly set, it soaks into the buttered bread. The crusts on the bread that emerge golden, glazed and chewy are the best bit, and a coarse-textured white or rye bread will be well-rewarded. A day's staling provides just the right texture, nothing too fresh, the aim is a crumb that can hold its custard. A salty butter isn't a bad idea either, a good Breton one set with fine crystals of sea salt that crunch as you eat them.

marmalade bread and butter pudding

Salted butter, softened
6 thin slices day-old white
    bread, with crusts
150g coarse-cut marmalade
300ml double cream
300ml fresh orange juice
8 medium egg yolks
100g golden caster sugar

Serves 6

Butter the slices of bread on one side and spread with marmalade. Cut them into 2 triangles and lay these in two rows of overlapping slices, marmalade-side up, along the length of a 35cm (2.5 litre) oval gratin or other shallow ovenproof dish. Arrange the rows at an angle to each other so the surface is even.

Pour the cream and orange juice into a small pan and bring to the boil. Whisk the egg yolks and sugar in a small bowl, then whisk on the hot cream and orange mixture and return to the pan. Gently heat, stirring constantly and covering the base of the pan with a wooden spoon, until the custard thickens enough to coat the back of it. Pour this through a sieve over the bread, as evenly as possible. Gently press down with the spoon to coat the bread thoroughly and leave to stand for 15 minutes.

Preheat the oven to 180°C fan/200°C/gas mark 6. Place the gratin dish in a roasting pan with warm water that comes two-thirds of the way up the sides and bake for 30–35 minutes until the custard has set on top, the edges of the bread are golden and crisp, and the marmalade sticky and glazed. Serve 5–10 minutes out of the oven.

In essence this is an old-fashioned bread and butter pudding, with a wobbly egg custard that's puffy and golden. But from there we depart to panettone, which contains an artful mix of dried fruits and candied peel and so does away with the need for raisins and the like, though that's not to say that you can't play it the old-fashioned way. For a traditional bread and butter pud, scatter 50g of sultanas and raisins over the base of the dish, soaked in rum if wished, and replace the panettone with triangles of day-old white bread.

buttered panettone pudding

3 medium eggs
150g golden caster sugar
425ml double cream
425ml milk
Softened unsalted butter for spreading
10–12 x 1cm slices panettone, cut as wedges from a 500g loaf,
1 vanilla pod
90g apricot jam, warmed and sieved (optional)

Serves 6

Preheat the oven to 160°C fan/180°C/gas mark 4. Whisk the eggs and sugar in a bowl, then whisk in the cream and milk. Butter the panettone and arrange in overlapping slices to cover the base of a 35cm (2.5 litre) oval gratin or other shallow ovenproof dish. The centre of an oval dish may take two slices side by side; the narrow ends may only hold one. Pour the custard through a sieve over and around the panettone. Tuck the vanilla pod beneath the custard in the centre.

Place the gratin dish in a roasting pan with cold water that comes two-thirds of the way up the sides. Bake for 1 hour until the custard is puffy and set and the bread golden. Brush the surface of the bread with the apricot jam; this bit is optional but it gives the pudding a lovely sticky glaze. Serve immediately. The vanilla pod can be rinsed and used again.

A cooling ambrosial creamed rice to dish up with whatever fruits are in season; my choice would be pomegranate seeds in the depths of winter and some slivers of peach in summer. The more vanilla you can run to the better: one pod is a treat and two a joy, the rice should be liberally flecked with minute black seeds. And I favour risotto over pudding rice – it's much better at retaining its texture and shape. In boffin-speak, both are short grain and belong to the Japonica family that includes sticky and sushi rice; the starch is altogether different from that found in basmati and other long grain rice. Of the various risotto rices, arborio does an excellent job.

vanilla creamed rice

Rice

150g arborio risotto rice

425ml full-cream milk

25g unsalted butter

50g caster sugar

1 vanilla pod

Custard

2 medium egg yolks

60g caster sugar

200ml full-cream milk

150g crème fraîche

Seeds from 1 pomegranate, to serve

Serves 6

Preheat the oven to 200°C fan/220°C/gas mark 7. Bring a medium ovenproof pan of water to the boil, add the rice and boil for 5 minutes, then drain.

Place the milk, butter and sugar for the rice in the same pan and bring to the boil. Add the vanilla pod and stir in the drained rice. Return the milk to a simmer, cover the rice with a circle of baking paper and then the lid. Place the pan in the oven, lower the temperature to 130°C fan/150°C/gas mark 3 and cook for about 40 minutes until the rice has absorbed all the milk. Remove the pan from the oven, take out and reserve the vanilla pod and allow the rice to cool.

While the rice is cooking, make the custard. Whisk together the egg yolks and sugar until pale. Bring the milk to the boil in a small pan, beat it into the egg mixture, then pour it back into the pan and cook over a very low heat until the mixture thickens and coats the back of a spoon, without allowing it to boil. Strain the custard through a sieve into a bowl or jug. Open out the reserved vanilla pod and run a small sharp knife down its length to scrape out the seeds. Stir these into the custard, cover the surface with clingfilm and leave to cool.

Combine the cooled rice with the custard and stir in the crème fraîche. Cover and chill for several hours or overnight. The rice is nicest eaten 30 minutes out of the fridge. Serve a mound of rice with the pomegranate seeds spooned over.

So named because of the surprise that lies below the souffléd top, though I have slightly deviated from the original here, baking it in a water bath which creates a lovely lightly set custard below as opposed to a sauce. Some runny cream is welcome.

lemon surprise pudding

115g unsalted butter, diced
150g golden caster sugar
Zest and juice of 2 lemons
4 medium eggs, separated
25g plain flour
500ml milk

Serves 6

Preheat the oven to 170°C fan/190°C/gas mark 5. Place the butter, sugar and lemon zest in the bowl of a food processor and cream together until light and fluffy. Incorporate the egg yolks one by one, and then the lemon juice and the flour. Add the milk, with the motor running.

Transfer the mixture to a large bowl. Whisk the egg whites until they are stiff; I use a hand-held electric whisk, and fold or whisk them in two goes into the lemon mixture. Pour this into a buttered 30cm (2 litre) oval gratin or other shallow ovenproof dish, at least 5cm deep. Place this inside a roasting dish with warm water that comes two-thirds of the way up the sides of the dish and bake for 40–45 minutes until golden and risen like a soufflé. Serve immediately.

Clafoutis Limousin is one of the few puddings in the true sense of the word that the French go in for – juicy black cherries baked in a surround of sweetened batter. It can be made with all manner of fruits, but prunes that have been slowly simmered in rum are a particular treat. It's yummiest eaten hot or lukewarm, about 30 minutes out of the oven, and I'm happy with a slice eaten in the hand with a napkin, but there are no rules against bowls and jugs of cream either.

prune clafoutis

Batter

75g plain flour, sifted

50g caster or vanilla sugar,
   plus extra for dusting the dish

3 medium eggs

425ml milk

25g unsalted butter, plus extra
   for greasing the dish

Prunes

150ml dark rum, plus 1 tablespoon

150ml water

50g caster or vanilla sugar

200g prunes, ready-soaked
   and stoned

Icing sugar for dusting

Serves 4–6

First make the batter as it needs to rest. Put the flour, sugar, eggs and milk in a liquidiser and blend them until smooth and creamy. Set aside for 30 minutes. If making the batter by hand, you will probably need to give it a whisk at the end.

Put the 150ml rum, the water and sugar for the prunes in a small pan and bring to the boil. Add the prunes and simmer for 15–25 minutes until all the liquid has been absorbed and they are coated in a sticky syrup.

Preheat the oven to 200°C fan/220°C/gas mark 7. Butter a 35cm (2.5 litre) gratin dish and dust with caster or vanilla sugar, tipping out the excess. Pour in the batter, then scatter the prunes and syrup evenly over the surface. Dot with the butter and bake for 25–30 minutes. When it comes out of the oven it will be impressively puffed and golden, sinking after a few minutes. Sprinkle over the remaining tablespoon of rum. Dust with icing sugar just before serving.

vanilla sugar

To make vanilla sugar, cut up a vanilla pod and whizz with 225g caster sugar in a food processor, then pass through a sieve. Store in a jar and use as required.

Seriously indulgent: the calorie-conscious should switch off now. This comes with a fluffy suet crust and a lavish pool of brown sugar and butter sauce scented with lemon inside. Only the hardy need eat the 'frog' – the lemon – the crust and sauce are the best bits, but be sure to scrape out the lemon flesh from the skin.

sussex pond pudding

Combine the flour, breadcrumbs, lemon zest, suet and salt in a large bowl, and add just enough milk to bring the dough together. Set aside about a quarter of the dough for the lid, and roll the remainder into a 25cm circle on a lightly floured work surface, and use to line a 1 litre pudding basin, folding over any pleats and pressing them into the side. Trim the top. Place half the butter and sugar in the bottom. Roll the lemon on the worksurface and prick it all over with a skewer, nestle it on top of the butter and sugar, then place the remaining butter and sugar around the sides. Roll out the remaining dough with any trimmings, brush the rim of the dough in the bowl with milk and place the lid on top, pressing the edges together to seal them, then trim the edge. Don't worry if there appears to be a little space below the lid, the sides will swell as it cooks.

Place a circle of baking paper over the basin and tie it in position using string. Place the pudding basin in a pan with boiling water that comes halfway up the sides, cover and cook over a low heat for 2½ hours, replenishing the water as necessary.

Remove the baking paper, run a knife around the edge of the pudding, place a deep plate on top and invert it. Serve in wedges with the buttery sauce that spills out.

120g self-raising flour, sifted
100g fresh white breadcrumbs
finely grated zest of 1 lemon, plus 1
    whole lemon (stalk removed)
120g shredded suet
Pinch of sea salt
About 90ml milk
100g unsalted butter, diced
100g light muscovado sugar

Serves 4–6

I love the way recipes evolve with the person who cooks them, and this is a friend Val Archer's take on Karen Perry's Danish apple cake. Not conventionally baked, alternate layers of crisp breadcrumbs are layered with an apple compote, before being chilled. And it is one of the most soothing puddings I have had, not too sweet or rich.

brown sugar apple cake

Purée

1.5kg Bramley apples, peeled,
    cored and sliced
Finely grated zest of 1 lemon, and
    juice of ½ lemon
75g demerara sugar
75g sultanas
3 cloves
1 teaspoon vanilla extract

Crumb layer

120g unsalted butter
270g dry white breadcrumbs
75g ground almonds
120g golden granulated sugar
Few drops of almond essence

50g toasted almonds (see page 97)
Icing sugar for dusting
Whipped cream or vanilla ice cream
    to serve (optional)

Makes 1 x 20cm cake
Serves 6–8

Place the apples in a large pan with the lemon zest and juice and add just enough water to prevent the fruit from catching on the bottom, only to a depth of a few millimetres. Add the sugar, sultanas, cloves and vanilla, bring to the boil, then cover and cook over a low heat for 10–20 minutes until soft, stirring halfway through. If the apples are sitting in a lot of juice, simmer to reduce it. You should end up with a chunky purée. Discard the cloves.

You need to cook the crumbs in two goes. Melt half the butter in a large frying pan over a medium heat, add half the breadcrumbs and half the ground almonds and fry, stirring almost constantly until lightly golden and crisp. Add half the sugar once the crumbs begin to colour. Transfer to a bowl and cook the remaining half of the ingredients in the same way. Stir in a few drops of almond essence.

Scatter a quarter of the breadcrumb mixture over the base of a 20cm cake tin at least 4cm deep with a removeable base. Spread a third of the apple purée on top, then two more layers of crumbs and apples, finishing with crumbs. Chill uncovered for 6–8 hours, or overnight.

To serve, run a knife around the collar of the tin and remove it. Scatter the cake with the toasted almonds and dust with icing sugar. Accompany with whipped cream or vanilla ice cream if wished. It is at its best chilled, and eaten within a day while the crumbs on top are still crisp, though it will be tasty for several days afterwards.

Strains of summer pudding here, bread toasted to a buttery crisp in the oven, soaking up the juices of a warm berry compote. A dollop of clotted cream hovers as an idea above it.

berry charlotte

800g mixture of raspberries
   and blackberries
200g redcurrants, strung
1 tablespoon plain flour
150g caster sugar
6 thin slices white bread
Softened unsalted butter for spreading

Serves 6

Preheat the oven to 180°C fan/200°C/gas mark 6. Combine the berries and currants in a large bowl, sprinkle over the flour and sugar and toss to combine. Tip the mixture into a 30 x 20cm baking dish.

Cut off the crusts from the bread, squaring the slices. Butter them on both sides and cut each slice into 4 triangles. Lay these in three overlapping rows on top of the fruit and bake for 30–35 minutes until the bread is golden and crisp on the surface and the fruit is bubbling. Leave to stand for 10 minutes before serving.

To me, this one has the appearance of the kind of luscious dessert that you might offer up had you been a farmer's wife in America's Mid-West during the gold rush, and I couldn't resist including it. It lies somewhere in between a cheesecake and a sponge, set with big juicy red cherries.

cherry cheesecake cake

Base

75ml white wine
150g golden caster sugar
¼ teaspoon bicarbonate of soda
2 medium eggs
60ml groundnut oil
1 teaspoon vanilla extract
100g self-raising flour, sifted

Topping

250g sour cream
50g icing sugar
150g cherries, pitted

Makes 1 x 20cm cake
Serves 6–8

Preheat the oven to 160°C fan/180°C/gas mark 4 and lightly oil the inside of a 20cm cake tin, at least 5cm deep, with a removeable base.

Heat the wine and half the sugar in a small pan over a lowish heat, stirring until the sugar melts, then stir in the bicarbonate of soda and set aside for about 20 minutes.

Whisk the remaining sugar with one of the eggs, the oil and vanilla in a bowl, then stir in the flour and wine mixture, half at a time, alternately. Transfer the cake mixture to the prepared tin and bake for 25 minutes until firm and shrinking from the sides.

Increase the temperature to 180°C fan/200°C/gas mark 6. Whisk the sour cream with the icing sugar in a bowl, then whisk in the remaining egg. Smooth this over the surface of the cake, scatter over the cherries and return to the oven for about 25 minutes until the filling is golden at the edges. Leave it to cool, then run a knife around the edge of the cake and remove the collar to serve.

A tart that kills on looks, from Baking with Passion by Dan Lepard and Richard Whittington – recipes from the wonderful patisserie Baker and Spice: it tastes divine too. They do of course make their own puff pastry, and you don't have to, but do try to find one made with butter and not vegetable fat – check out the freezer section.

plum and frangipane tart

225g puff pastry

9 slightly under-ripe Victoria plums,
  quartered and stoned

3 tablespoons apricot jam, warmed
  and sieved

Frangipane

200g softened unsalted butter

150g caster sugar

125g ground almonds

125g ground hazelnuts*

100g plain flour

3 medium eggs

**Makes 1 x 25cm tart
Serves 6–8**

Preheat the oven to 180°C fan/200°C/gas mark 6. Make the frangipane first. Blend the butter with the sugar in a food processor for about 8 minutes. Add the ground nuts and flour and beat briefly, then whisk in the eggs, one at a time. Set the frangipane aside.

Roll out the pastry into a thin circle on a lightly floured surface, and cut out a round to fit a 25cm tin. Use the rolling pin to gently lift the pastry into the tin and press it into the bottom and the sides. Run the pin across the top to trim.

Spread the frangipane over the pastry base, and arrange the plum quarters cut-side up on top, laying them in circles starting at the outside. Bake for 15 minutes, then reduce the temperature to 140°C fan/160°C/gas mark 3 and bake for a further 35–45 minutes by which time the frangipane will have risen up around the plums and set. Brush the surface of the tart with the warmed jam and leave to cool.

* While you can buy ready-ground almonds, you will need to grind your own hazelnuts in an electric coffee grinder. Alternatively substitute ground almonds.

Crema Catalana is the Spanish equivalent of crème brûlée, every bit as silky and sinful, here served as a tart filling on a buttery biscuit base.

custard tart

Custard

3 gelatine leaves (e.g. Supercook, cut into broad strips (or ¾ sachet powdered gelatine, see page 47)
600ml single cream
125g caster sugar
1 cinnamon stick
2 strips lemon zest
6 medium organic egg yolks
Icing sugar for dusting

Almond Crust

100g flaked almonds, toasted (see page 97)
180g sweet buttery biscuits (e.g. Fox's Butter Crunch Crinkles) or shortbread
40g unsalted butter

Makes 1 x 20cm tart
Serves 6–8

Place the gelatine strips in a bowl, cover with cold water and soak for 5 minutes, then drain. Put the cream, sugar, cinnamon and lemon zest in a small non-stick pan and bring almost to the boil, stirring occasionally so the sugar melts. Whisk this onto the egg yolks in a bowl, it will thicken instantly into a thin custard. Pour a little over the gelatine, stir to dissolve, then add it back to the rest of the custard. Pass through a sieve, then cover and leave to cool, and chill for 3–4 hours until semi-set.

Meanwhile, preheat the oven to 180°C fan/200°C/gas mark 6. Briefly whizz half the toasted almonds in a food processor to coarsely chop, then remove. Break up the biscuits and whizz to crumbs, again in the food processor. Gently melt the butter in a small pan over a low heat, tip in the crumbs and chopped almonds and stir to coat them. Press the mixture into the base of a 20cm cake tin 9cm deep with a removeable base, and chill it.

Spoon the semi-set custard over the biscuit base, smoothing the surface with the back of a spoon, then cover and chill overnight. Remove from the fridge 15 minutes before serving. Scatter the remaining almonds over the top and liberally dust with icing sugar. Run a knife around the collar of the tin and remove it. Serve in slices.

Summer pudding consists of a shell of white bread soaked in dramatically dark, sultry crimson juices encasing a compote: unlikely but true. It may have been invented as a healthy alternative to richer 18th-century offerings, though not with a dollop of clotted cream. For a connoisseur's pud it's surprising how rarely you come across a really good one. While it's not difficult to get right, it's easy to get it wrong. The bread should be a loaf of day-old white bread and the slices must be used to line the basin as seamlessly as possible – any cracks will allow the juice to seep out once the pudding has been inverted.

summer pudding

225g redcurrants

225g blackcurrants

170g caster sugar

700g raspberries, blackberries or loganberries

¾ unsliced loaf of day-old white bread, sliced by hand ¾cm thick (you need 8–10 slices)

Clotted cream to serve

Serves 6

String the currants into a small pan using a fork, add the sugar and heat together for 4–5 minutes until the fruit is soft but still retains its shape, and is sitting in a pool of syrup. Place half the currants in a sieve and press the juice into a bowl and then return it to the pan, discarding the solids. Fold in the other berries, stir well and heat very gently for a minute or two, not to cook them but to encourage them to release their juices. Leave the fruit to cool, then adjust the sweetness if necessary with a little more sugar. Set aside about two-thirds of a teacup of the fruit and juice, cover and put in the fridge.

Remove the crusts from the bread and line a 1.8 litre pudding basin. Place a square of bread on the base of the basin with four pieces around the sides, and fill in the triangular gaps as neatly as possible. Tip the fruit into the basin and press it down well using a wooden spoon. Make a lid with more bread, and trim the top of the sides in line. Place a small plate over the top, slightly smaller than the diameter of the pudding basin, and put a weight on top (unopened cans are ideal). Leave the pudding in the fridge overnight.

To serve, run a knife carefully round the edge of the pudding to loosen it, and then invert the pudding on to a plate. Leave the pudding to stand for 30–60 minutes, which will bring it back up to room temperature as well as allow the juices to soak into the base. Spoon the reserved fruit and juices over, soaking any bits of bread that haven't turned red. Serve it with plenty of clotted cream.

festive

Christmas and Easter are times when we throw off our shackles and call up all the good things in life. We can relax and linger at the table, eat a little bit more and drink a little bit more, and stop rushing. The chances are there will be plenty of takers for any puddings, festive or otherwise, which is good news for the cook as they rarely come in half sizes and you want lots of eager diners to do them justice.

There are scents and flavours that we hope and expect to find at these times of year, ones that we associate with our childhood, which immediately bring the memories flooding back. At Christmas it's a mass of dried fruits and candied peel, warming spices such as cinnamon, a grating of nutmeg, a hint of cloves and the rasp of brandy and rum. Whether they're woven into a Christmas pudding or a mince tart, they are as evocative as the scent of pine needles and wood smoke.

At Easter, we play with the same spices, a lighter touch with the fruit and candied peel perhaps, and more in the way of colour. We may not have the same traditional greats at this time of year, but a bread and butter pudding made with hot cross buns, a creamy charlotte with a cassata-like heart, or a bakewell tart all seem to herald primroses and violets in the banks and blackthorn in blossom in the hedgerows, picked out by a clear blue sky. And, of course, chocolate in any guise will be wolfed down, regardless of all those eggs on the sideboard.

Both the roulade and the remaining cranberry purée can be frozen, which helps your advance Christmas planning. Wrap the roulade in the paper, pop it inside a large freezer bag and freeze. Given its delicacy, I prefer to remove the paper first and leave it loosely covered with plastic on a plate to thaw for a couple of hours before serving.

cranberry ripple roulade

500g cranberries
350g caster sugar (refined)
Icing sugar for dusting
5 medium egg whites, at room temperature
300ml whipping cream

Serves 6–8

Place the cranberries in a medium pan with 100g of the sugar, cover and cook over a medium-low heat for 10–15 minutes, stirring halfway through, until the berries are soft and surrounded by juice. Press the cranberries and juice through a sieve, then return the purée to the pan and simmer to reduce it by about half, stirring towards the end. Pour it into a bowl, cover and leave to cool, then chill it for about an hour before you start the roulade.

Preheat the oven to 180°C fan /200°C/gas mark 6. Butter and line a 32 x 22cm Swiss roll tin with baking paper. Cut out a sheet of baking paper, 42 x 32cm, and dust lightly with icing sugar. Whisk the egg whites in a large bowl until stiff, then sprinkle over a tablespoon of the remaining sugar at a time, whisking well with each addition, until you have a stiff, glossy meringue; I use a hand-held electric whisk. Spoon it into the tin, and level. Place in the oven, reduce the heat to 140°C fan/160°C/gas mark 3 and bake for 15 minutes until lightly golden and firm when pressed.

Run a knife around the edge of the meringue and turn out onto the baking paper. Leave to cool to room temperature for 15–20 minutes. Whip the cream until it forms fluffy but firm peaks. Stir the cranberry purée to thin it, then spoon a third over the surface of the cream and fold it over a couple of times to marble it. Remove the top paper from the meringue, spoon the cream down the centre and smooth it over the top using a palette knife, leaving a rim. Now roll the roulade up, from a short end, using the baking paper underneath to help. Place on a plate and chill until required. Liberally dust with icing sugar shortly before eating, and serve in slices with the remaining purée drizzled over.

Still dreaming of white Christmases? This snow-clad mountain, a close relation to a *bûche de noël*, conceals a heart of chocolate chestnut cream. For the full Christmas schmaltz, you could adorn the sides with little trees and skiers.

snowy mountain

Centre

100g dark chocolate
   (about 70% cocoa), broken up
50g unsalted butter, diced
1 x 435g tin unsweetened
   chestnut purée
75g golden caster sugar
100ml extra thick double cream
1 teaspoon vanilla extract

Frosting

1 medium egg
75g icing sugar, sifted
25g plain flour, sifted
150ml full-cream milk
½ teaspoon vanilla extract
90g unsalted butter, softened

To decorate

Grated white chocolate
Icing sugar, for dusting

Serves 6–8

Place the chocolate and butter in a bowl set over a pan of simmering water and gently melt, stirring now and again until smooth and amalgamated. Set aside to cool: the chocolate needs to be at room temperature for the next stage.

Place the chestnut purée, sugar, cream and vanilla in the bowl of a food processor and whizz until creamy. Add the cooled chocolate and whizz again until you have a silky purée the consistency of whipped butter icing – firm enough to shape. If it seems a little loose, transfer the mixture to a bowl, cover and chill until it firms up.

Pile the mixture in the centre of a plate or cake board at least 20cm in diameter and shape into a cone. Put in the fridge to set for several hours, or overnight – in which case cover it after a few hours. To make the frosting, whisk the egg and icing sugar in a small non-stick pan until smooth, then whisk in the flour. Bring the milk to the boil in a small pan, and whisk it into the egg mixture. Cook the mixture over a low heat for a few minutes until the custard thickens, stirring vigorously with a wooden spoon to disperse any lumps. The custard shouldn't boil, but the odd bubble shows it's hot enough to thicken properly. Cook it for a few minutes longer, stirring constantly. Pass the custard through a sieve into a bowl, stir in the vanilla, cover the surface with clingfilm and leave to cool completely.

Beat the softened butter until light and creamy. Gradually whisk in the cooled custard; I use a hand-held electric whisk, then whisk for a few minutes, initially on low and then on a higher speed, until white and fluffy. Using a palette knife, smooth this over the chocolate cone. Pile grated chocolate on the crest to resemble newly fallen snow, and dust with icing sugar. Loosely cover with clingfilm and chill for a few hours. It keeps well for several days. I like to serve it about 30 minutes out of the fridge.

last-minute christmas pudding

I took great encouragement the first Christmas I dished this one up to my family from the fact that my mum, who has always made her Christmas puds months in advance, gave it the thumbs up over a traditional matured pud. Perhaps that's because it's lighter than the norm, and seems to slip down more easily.

You can make it in advance of the main course, and leave it standing in the pan. Equally though you can cook it a day or two in advance (or freeze and defrost it), and steam it for an hour to reheat. In this case remove the paper once it is cooked, cover it with clingfilm and put fresh paper on before rewarming. Whisk 1–2 tablespoons dark rum and 50g sifted icing sugar into 200g crème fraîche to make a boozy cream, or simply serve it plain.

100g raisins

100g sultanas

200g currants

100ml stout

4 tablespoons brandy

100g finely diced candied peel

50g finely chopped blanched almonds

50g undyed glacé cherries,
   coarsely chopped

½ teaspoon each ground cinnamon
   and nutmeg

125g unsalted butter

125g dark muscovado sugar

2 medium eggs

1 tablespoon treacle

180g self-raising flour, sifted

50ml milk

To serve

Rum cream (see introduction,
   opposite) or crème fraîche

Serves 6–8

Place the dried fruits in a small pan with the stout and brandy and gently simmer, stirring occasionally, until all the liquor has been absorbed. Transfer the fruit to a large mixing bowl and leave to cool for 20–30 minutes. Stir in the peel, almonds, cherries and spices.

Cream the butter and sugar together for several minutes in a food processor, then incorporate the eggs, one by one, then the treacle, the flour and finally the milk. Blend the cake mixture with the dried fruit mixture.

Butter a 1.2 litre pudding basin, line the bottom with baking paper and butter this also. Spoon the mixture into the pudding basin and smooth the surface. Cut out two circles of baking paper to cover the surface of the pudding, with several inches to spare on either side. Lay them on top of each other, pleated in the centre, butter the surface that will come into contact with the pudding and place over the top. Tightly tie the paper in place with string, just below the rim. Place in a large pan with boiling water that comes two-thirds of the way up the sides, cover and simmer over a low heat for $2^{1}/2$ hours. Check the water level now and again and top it up if necessary.

Run a knife around the rim of the pudding and invert onto a plate. Serve with the cream.

Baked Alaska has always spelled a grand finale, of the same era as crêpes suzettes and all things flambéed. But here the snowy mountain of warm marshmallow-like meringue conceals Christmas pudding, and cooling ice cream just beginning to melt. You might pop a little holly in the top, too.

christmas pudding alaska

1 x 500ml tub of vanilla
   (or other spice-flavoured) ice cream
1 x 450g Christmas pudding
4 medium egg whites
225g caster sugar

Serves 6

The trick is to have everything ready for the pudding in advance of dinner, so that it can be quickly assembled just before serving. Several hours before eating, remove the ice cream from the freezer and leave it to soften for 20 minutes. Then slice it across 1 cm thick, and lay the slices out on a small baking tray or a Swiss roll tin that will fit into the freezer. Loosely cover the ice cream with clingfilm and return to the freezer to harden.

About an hour before eating, place the Christmas pudding in a saucepan with water that comes a third of the way up its sides. Bring to the boil, then cover and simmer over a low heat for 1 hour. Remove from the heat and leave the pudding in the pan while you eat your main course.

The meringue will hold for up to 60 minutes, so you can either whisk it before you eat, or just before pudding. Preheat the oven to 220°C fan/240°C/gas mark 9. Whisk the egg whites in a large bowl until stiff. Gradually sprinkle over the sugar, whisking between each addition until you have a stiff and glossy meringue.

Turn out the hot Christmas pudding onto a board and slice it into about 8 wedges. Arrange these in two rows side by side on a baking sheet (covered with foil if you like), so the slices overlap like roof tiles. Ease the ice cream slices off the baking sheet using a palette knife and lay them on top, again in two rows. Smooth the meringue over the sides and top so the pudding and ice cream are completely concealed. Bake for 3–4 minutes until the meringue is set and turning a pale gold. Serve immediately from the baking tray.

This has a relaxed, rustic feel to it, a big slab of tart that can be cut any size you want, and there's no rolling out of pastry, which may find fans among you at the busy time of Christmas. The lemon and the apples cut through the sweetness of the mincemeat, and walnuts too are something in the way of distraction.

apple, walnut and mincemeat tart

Walnut Pastry

175g unsalted butter, diced
75g golden caster sugar
150g plain flour
1 teaspoon baking powder, sifted
100g walnut pieces
2 medium egg yolks

Mincemeat Top

Finely grated zest of 1 lemon
400g mincemeat
3 eating apples, peeled, cored and
   finely sliced into rings
50g unsalted butter
3 teaspoons golden caster sugar
50g apricot jam

Makes 12 slices

Preheat the oven to 180ºC fan/200ºC/gas mark 6 and butter a 30 x 23 x 4cm baking tin.

To make the walnut pastry, whizz the butter, sugar, flour, baking powder and walnuts in a food processor until the mixture starts to cling together, then add the egg yolks and continue to process to a sticky dough. Press this into the base of the cake tin, laying a sheet of clingfilm over the top and smoothing it with your fingers, then remove it. Bake for 15–20 minutes until lightly golden and slightly risen.

Stir the lemon zest into the mincemeat in a bowl, then smooth it over the shortcake base as evenly as possible; you may have small gaps here and there depending on the texture of the mincemeat. Lay the apple slices lengthwise in three overlapping rows, discarding the bottom slice, then dot with the butter and scatter over the sugar. Bake for 20–25 minutes until the edges of the apple slices have begun to colour. Remove and run a knife around the edge of the tart, then leave it to cool completely. Gently warm the jam, press it through a sieve and lightly brush the apple slices to glaze them, then leave to set.

Cut the tart into about 12 squares using a bread knife. You can either store the tart in the tin, covering it with clingfilm, or transfer the slices to an airtight container. They should keep well for several days.

Hot cross buns are full of dried fruit and spices and by Easter Monday, when you've had your fill of them for breakfast, they should be the perfect 'day-old' consistency for this classic old-fashioned bread and butter pudding.

hot cross bun pudding

3 medium eggs
150g golden caster sugar
425ml double cream
425ml milk
Salted butter for spreading

About 5–6 hot cross buns,
    sliced into 3 discs
1 vanilla pod
90g apricot jam, warmed and
    sieved (optional)

Serves 6

Preheat the oven to 160°C fan/180°C/gas mark 4. Whisk the eggs and sugar in a bowl, then whisk in the cream and milk. Select a 35cm (about 2.5 litre) oval gratin or other shallow ovenproof dish, that fits inside a roasting dish. Butter the hot cross bun slices, including the cross, and arrange, buttered-side up, fitting them into the dish as compactly as possible. Pour the custard through a sieve over and around the buns, and submerge the vanilla pod in the custard in the centre.

Place the gratin dish in a roasting pan with cold water that comes two-thirds of the way up the sides. Bake for 1 hour until the custard is puffy and set and the bread golden. Brush the surface of the bread with the apricot jam, this bit is optional but it gives the pudding a lovely sticky glaze. Serve immediately. The vanilla pod can be rinsed and used again.

This one spans festivities, it's great at Christmas as well as at Easter, and like all the best tarts, you can serve it for elevenses, tea or for pudding with a dollop of crème fraîche.

marzipan bakewell

Pastry

60g unsalted butter, softened

60g golden caster sugar

½ medium egg

125g plain flour, sifted

15g ground almonds

Filling

125g ready-made marzipan

50g unsalted butter, diced

75g golden caster sugar

2 medium eggs

120g ground almonds

½ teaspoon baking powder, sifted

50g raisins

100g raspberry jam

30g flaked almonds

Icing sugar for dusting

Serves 6–8

To make the pastry, cream the butter and sugar together in a food processor. Mix in the egg, then add the flour and ground almonds. As soon as the dough begins to form a ball, wrap it in clingfilm and chill for at least 2 hours; it can be kept in the fridge for several days.

Preheat the oven to 170°C fan/190°C/gas mark 5. Thinly roll out the pastry on a lightly floured surface and line the bottom and sides of a 23 x 3cm tart tin with a removeable base, trimming the excess. Don't worry if it tears and you end up partly pressing it into the tin. Line the case with baking paper and weight it with baking beans or dried pulses. Cook for 15–20 minutes until lightly coloured, then remove the paper and beans.

Meanwhile, thinly roll out the marzipan on a lightly floured surface, and cut out a 23cm circle. Cream the butter and sugar together in a food processor, then add the eggs one at a time, the ground almonds and baking powder. With the motor off, stir in the raisins. Lay the circle of marizpan over the base, spread with the raspberry jam, then spoon the almond sponge mixture on top, smoothing the surface. Scatter over the almonds and return to the oven for 25–30 minutes until golden and risen. The tart is delicious eaten 20–30 minutes out of the oven, otherwise leave to cool, then dust with icing sugar. The tart keeps well for several days in an airtight container.

A crisp shell with a gooey dark chocolate meringue inside, whipped cream streaked with chocolate on top and a few sugar-coated mini eggs to decorate. As lavish as it sounds.

chocolate pavlova

Pavlova

6 large egg whites, at room temperature
350g caster sugar
1 tablespoon cornflour, sifted
25g cocoa, sifted
1 teaspoon white wine vinegar

Top

100g milk chocolate, broken
  into pieces
300ml whipping cream, whipped

Sugar-coated mini eggs to decorate

Serves 6

Preheat the oven to 200°C fan/220°C/gas mark 7. Using a hand-held electric whisk, whip the egg whites in a bowl until they form stiff peaks, then scatter over the caster sugar a few tablespoons at a time, whisking well with each addition. Gradually whisk in the cornflour and cocoa, and then the vinegar, by which time you should have a very stiff, glossy meringue.

Cut out a circle of baking paper about 23cm in diameter and place this on a baking sheet. Spoon the mixture onto the circle, taking it almost to the edge of the paper, and swirl the top with the spoon. Place the pavlova in the oven, reduce the temperature to its very lowest setting (about 110°C fan/130°C/gas mark 1/2) and bake for 1 1/2 hours. Remove the pavlova from the oven, and leave it to cool. This needs to be made on the day it is to be eaten.

Gently melt the chocolate in a large bowl set over a pan with a little simmering water in it, then leave to cool to room temperature. Carefully tip the meringue onto its side, gently pull off the paper and place the pavlova on a large serving plate. Drizzle the chocolate over the whipped cream, and fold over a couple of times until it appears marbled. Spoon the cream into the centre of the pavlova. You can prepare it to this point up to an hour in advance, in which case chill it.

Pile some little eggs into the centre shortly before serving.

An Easter bonnet special, you could almost wear this one, with a centre something like a cassata.

easter charlotte

Finely grated zest of 1 lemon,
  plus the juice, sieved
75g caster sugar
75ml water
4 gelatine leaves (e.g. Supercook),
  cut into broad strips (or 1 sachet
  powdered gelatine, see page 47)
150ml double cream
⅔ packet of sponge fingers
  (about 130g)
750g ricotta, at room temperature
150g icing sugar
2 tablespoons dark rum
4 medium organic egg whites
75g candied mixed peel
Icing sugar for dusting
Edible paper roses or sugared violets
  to decorate*

Serves 6

Place the lemon juice and sugar in a small pan with the water, bring to the boil, stirring until the sugar dissolves, pour into a shallow bowl and leave to cool. Line the base of a 20cm soufflé dish with baking paper.

Place the gelatine strips in a bowl, cover with cold water and soak for 5 minutes, then drain. Gently heat the cream in a small pan until it feels hot to the touch, pour it over the soaked gelatine and stir to dissolve. Leave to cool to room temperature.

Briefly dip the underside of each sponge finger in the lemon syrup, and then use them to line the sides of the dish, standing them upright and placing them sugared-side out. Whizz the ricotta, cream, lemon zest, icing sugar and rum together in a food processor. Transfer the mixture to a large bowl. Whisk the egg whites in another large bowl until stiff; I use a hand-held electric whisk for this, and fold into the ricotta cream in two or three goes. Fold in the candied peel and fill the dish with the mixture, smoothing the surface. Cover with clingfilm and chill overnight.

To serve, place a plate on top of the dish and invert the pudding, then carefully peel off the paper. Dust with icing sugar and decorate with edible paper roses or sugared violets.

* Jane Asher's website is a boon for decorating this kind of pud – all manner of edible paper and sugared flowers can be ordered from www.jane-asher.co.uk.

index

acknowledgements

With very many thanks to Angela Mason, Food Editor on YOU Magazine, to Sue Peart, Editor, and John Koski, Associated Editor. Also to my agent Rosemary Sandberg at Ed Victor, to Stephanie Evans, Editor, Sophie Allen, Editorial Assistant, and to Kyle Cathie.